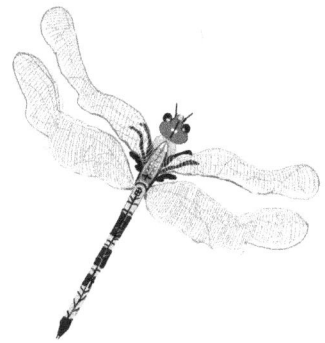

Art for Adults

A Collection of Flowers and Patterns to Color

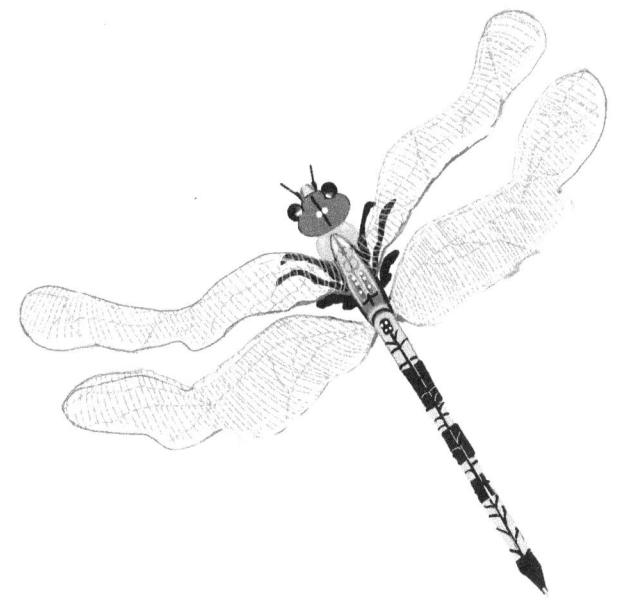

Illustrated by Ann Wyant

ISBN-13:978-1519260451
ISBN-10:1519260458

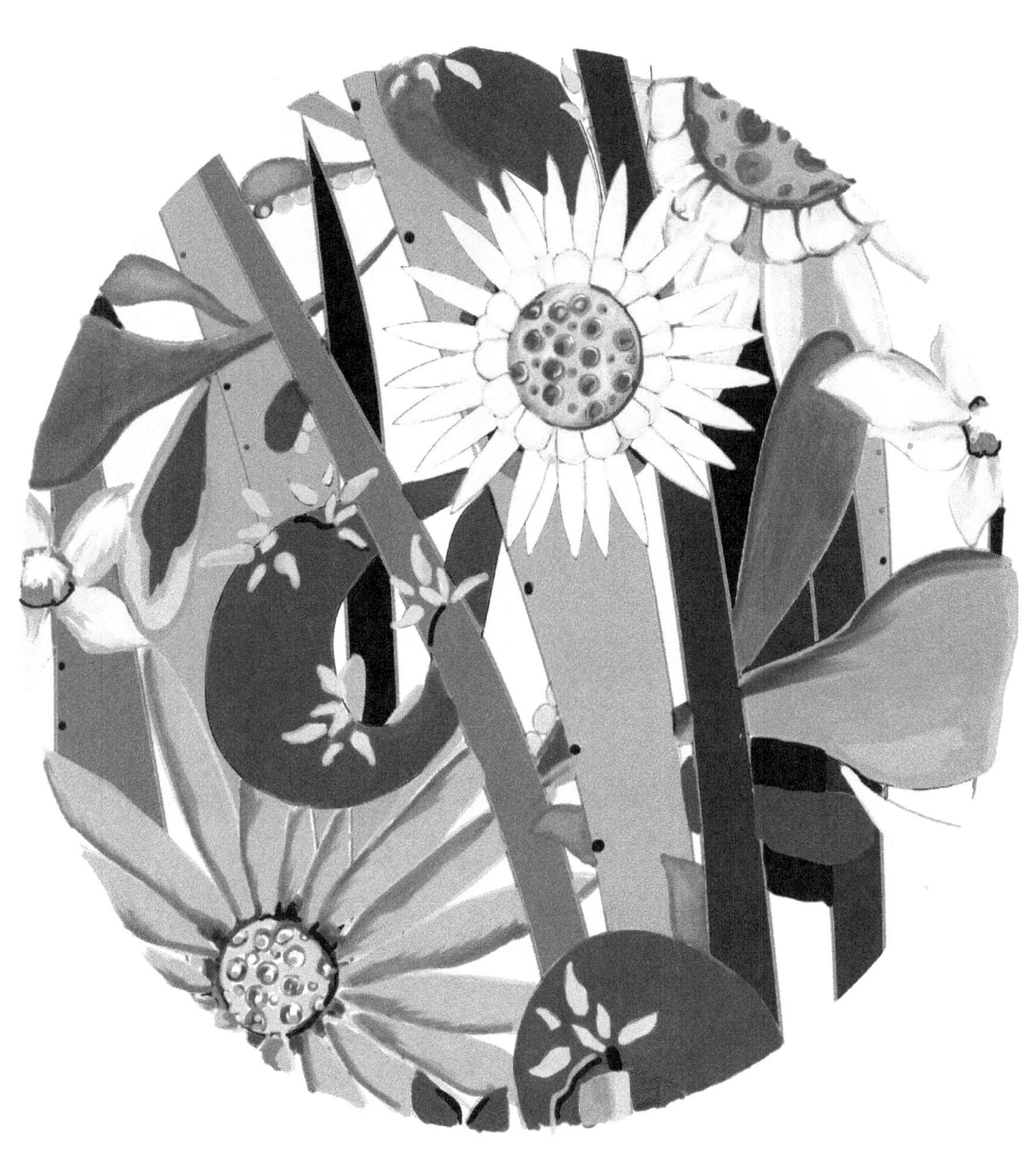

Art for Adults

Illustrated by Ann Wyant

Dedication

This book is dedicated to all the hard workers who need a break from daily stress.
My wish is to take you to a friendly colorful garden where you feel the peace and tranquility if only for a few minutes out of your busy day. Use colored pencils or crayons .

Enjoy coloring!

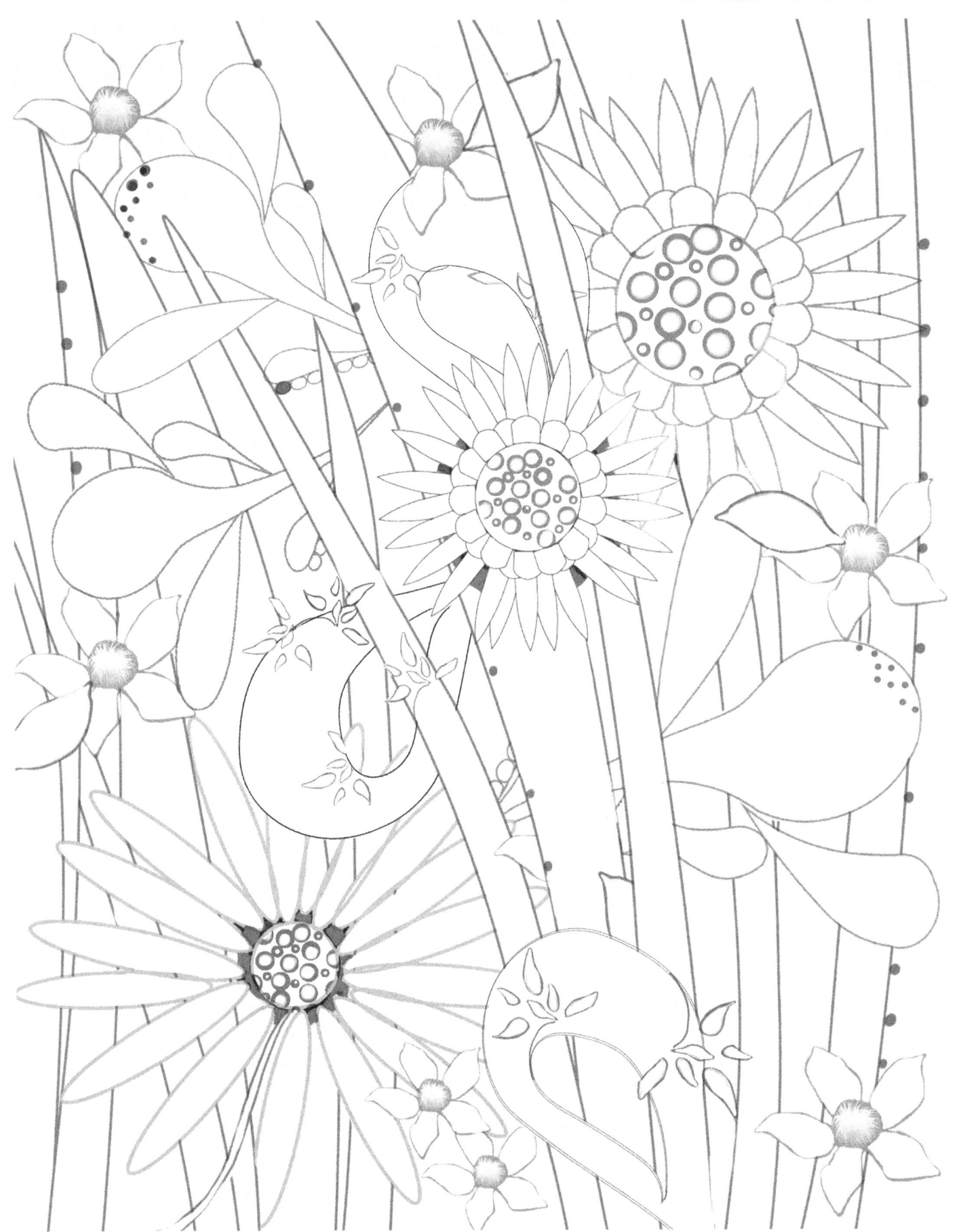

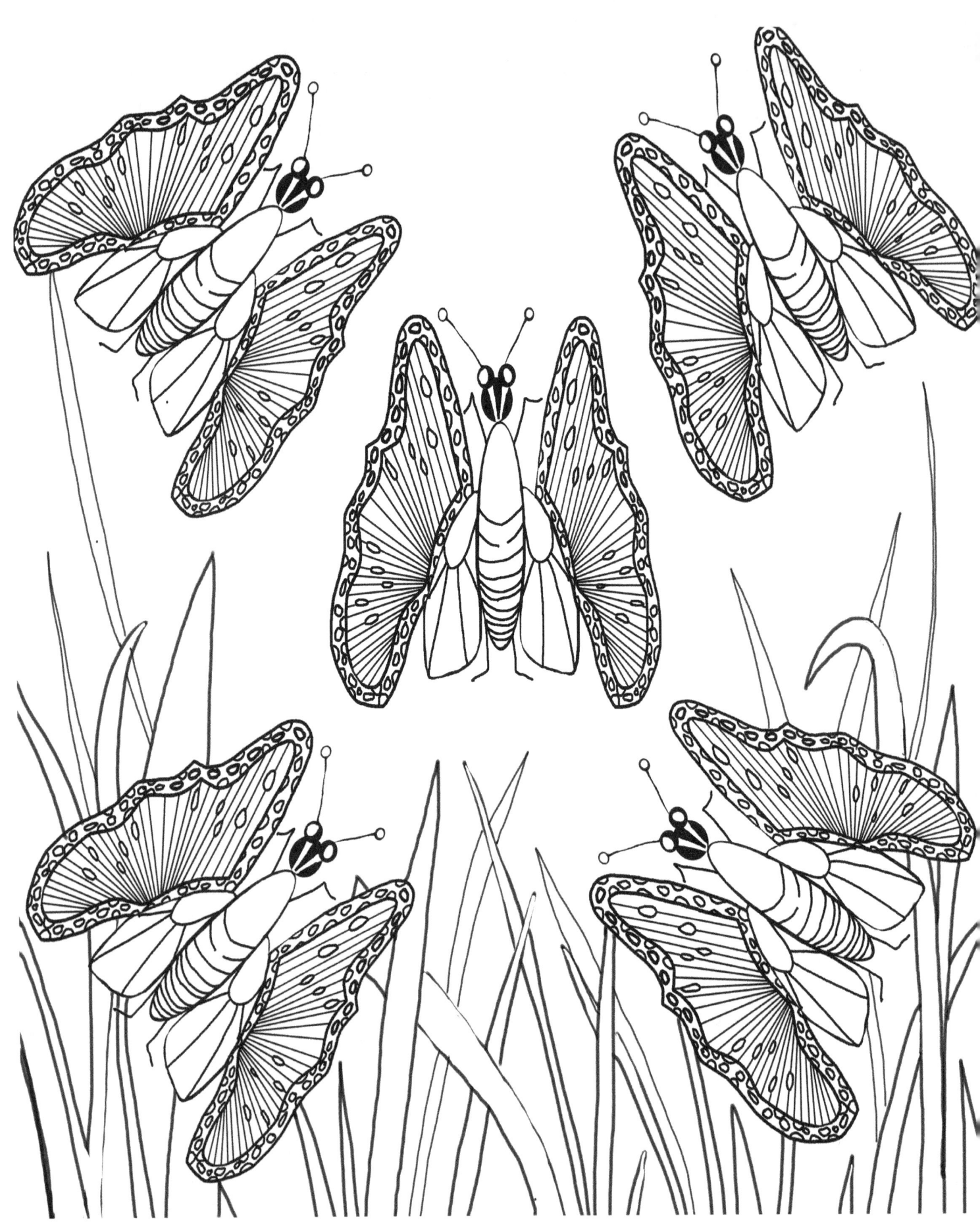

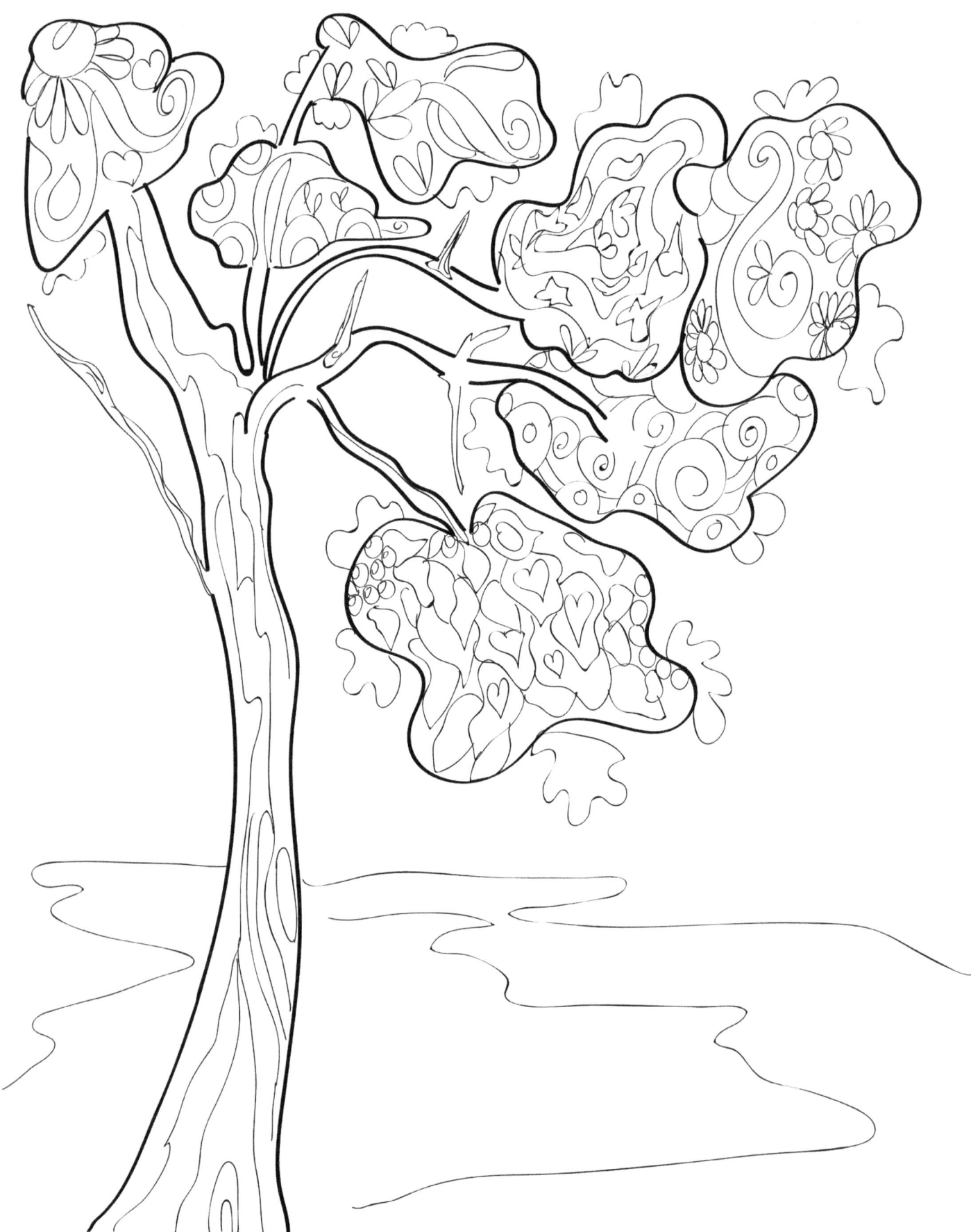

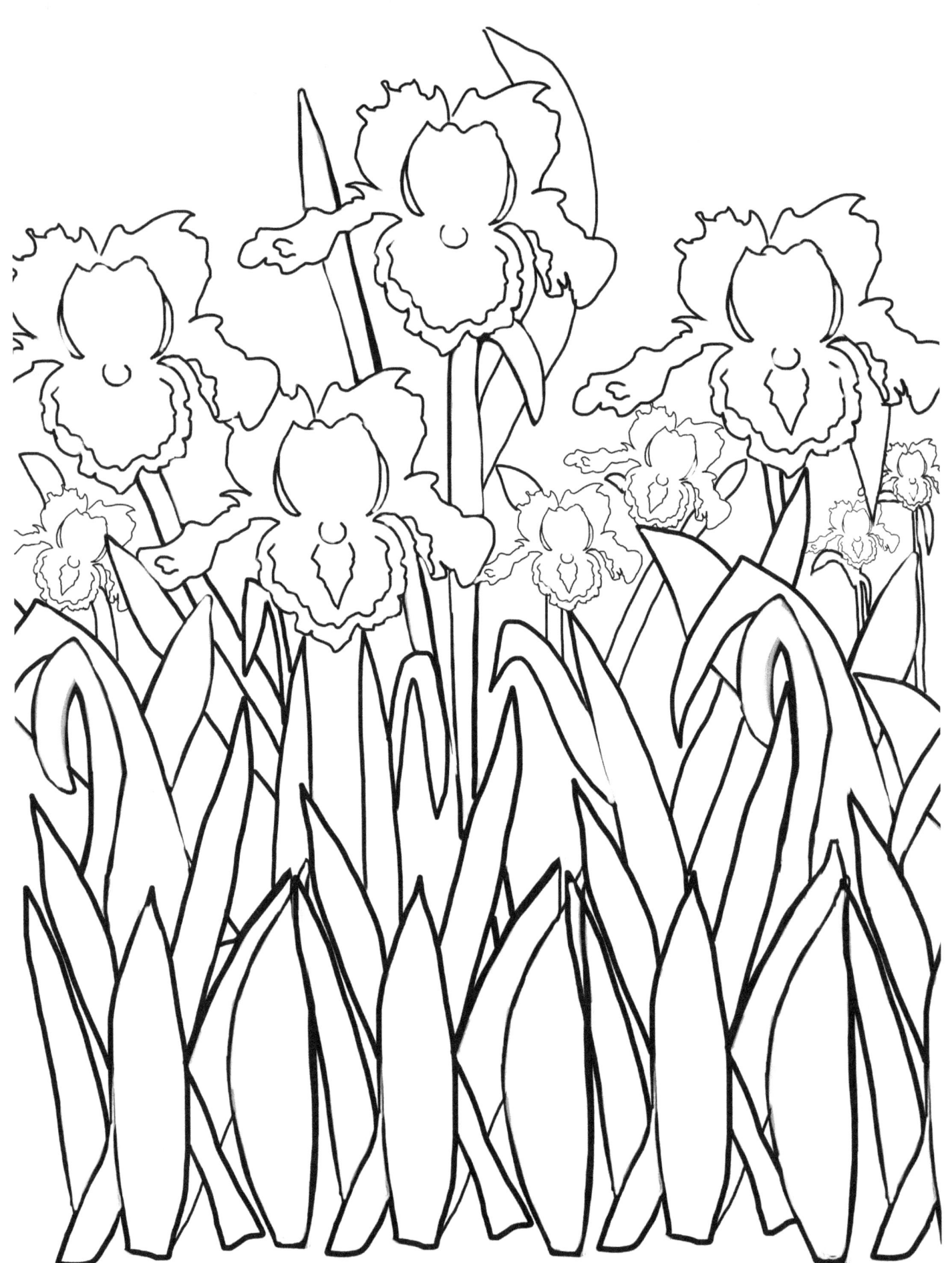

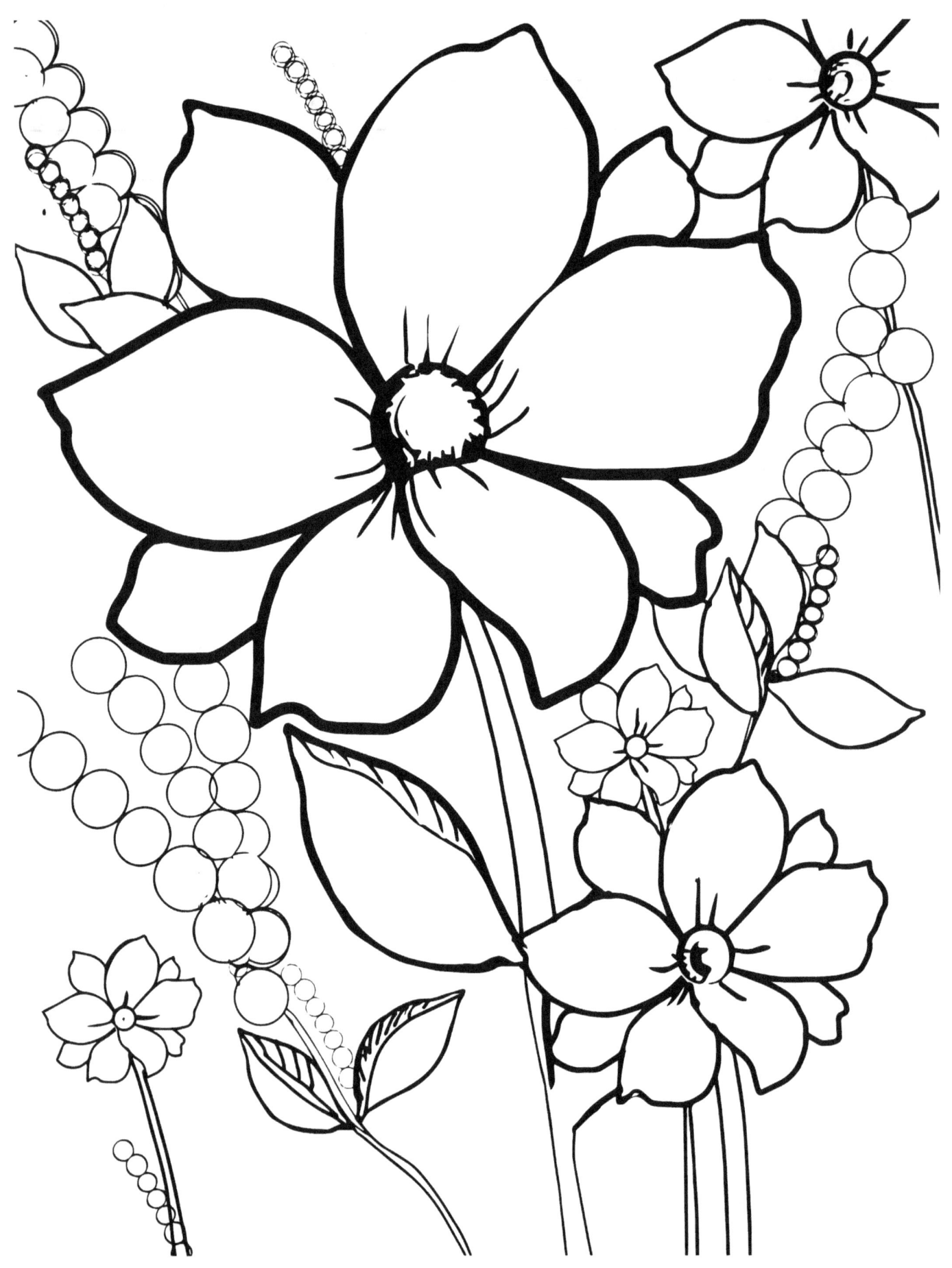

_____

_____

_____

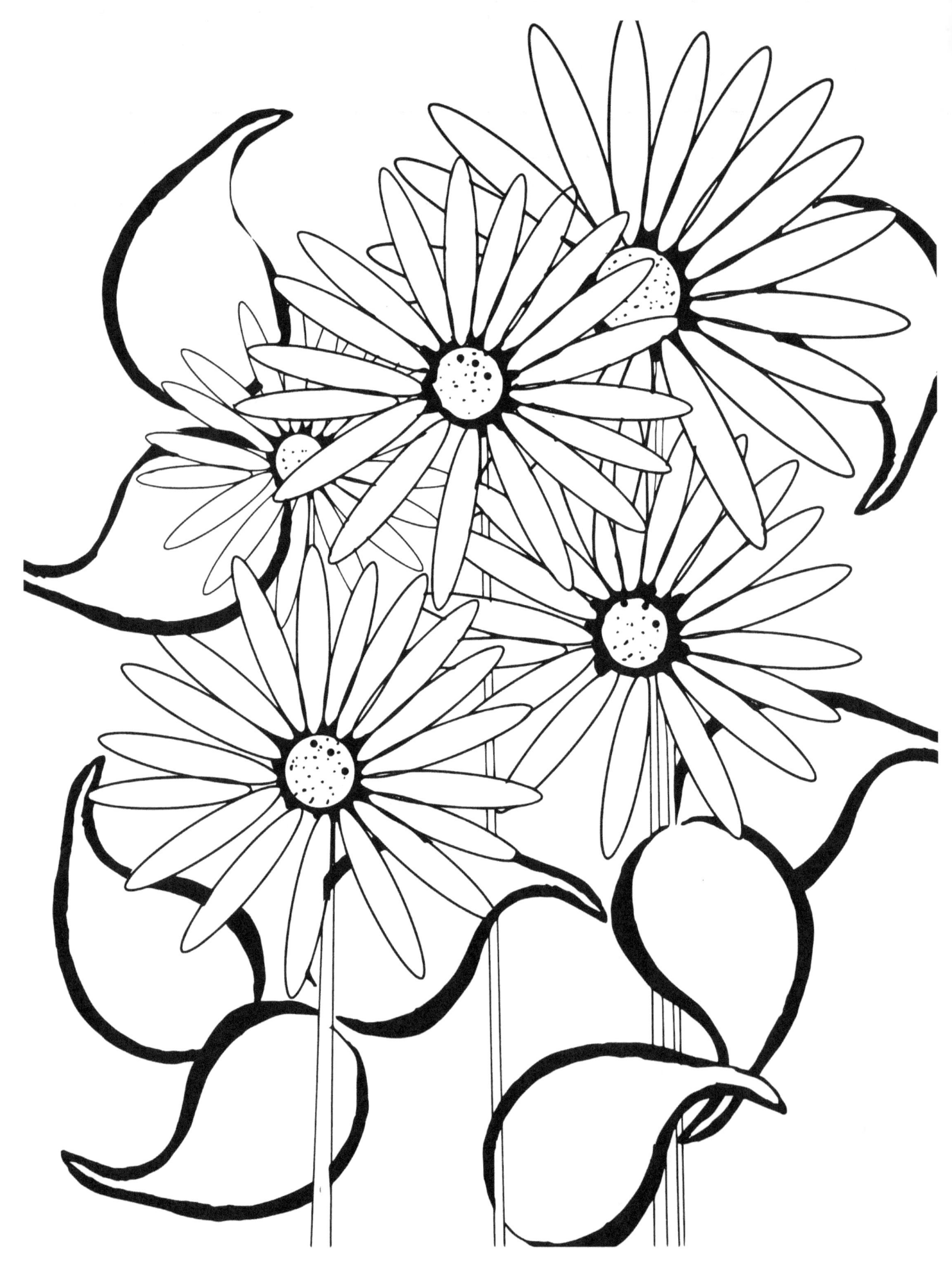

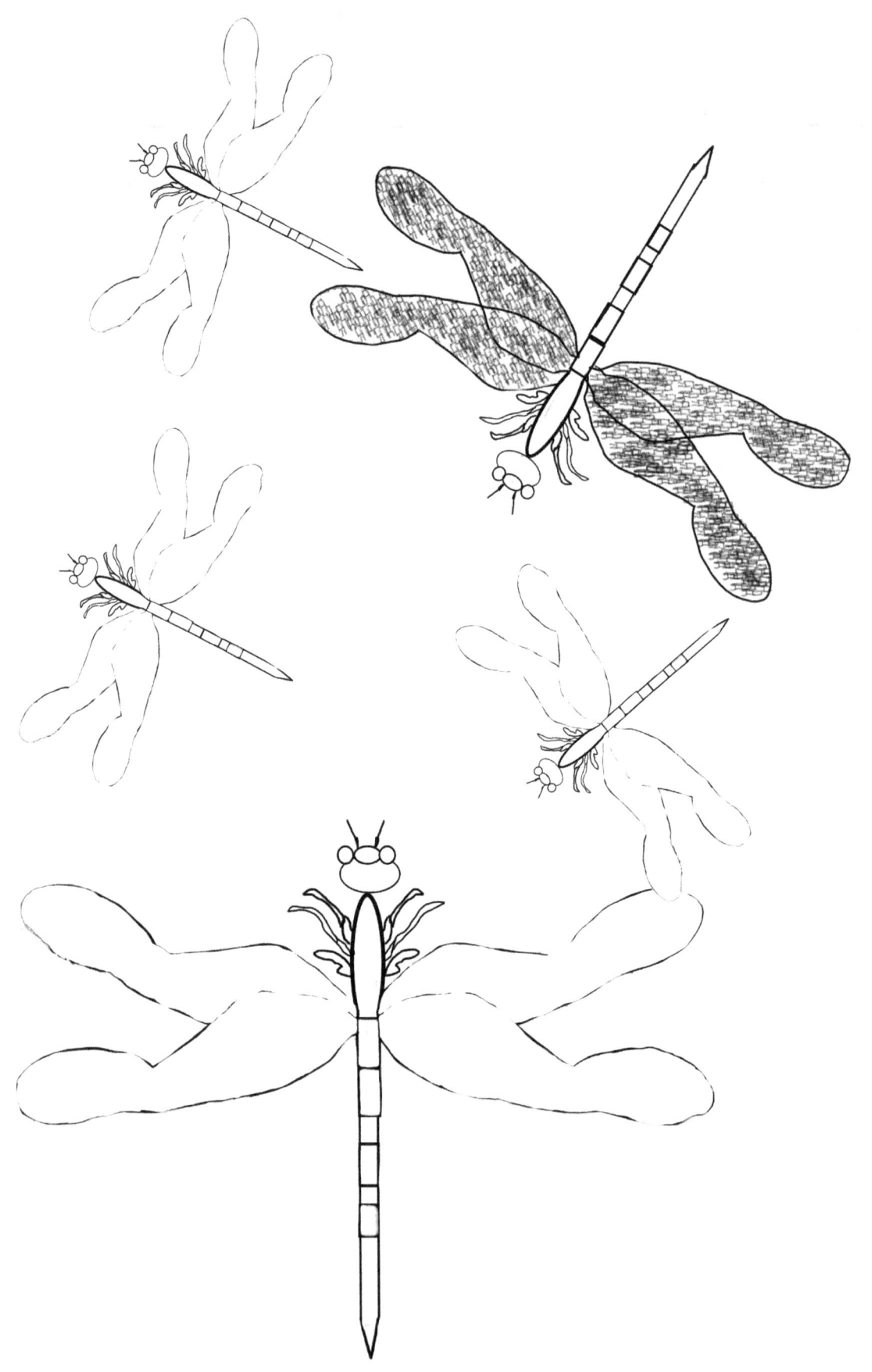

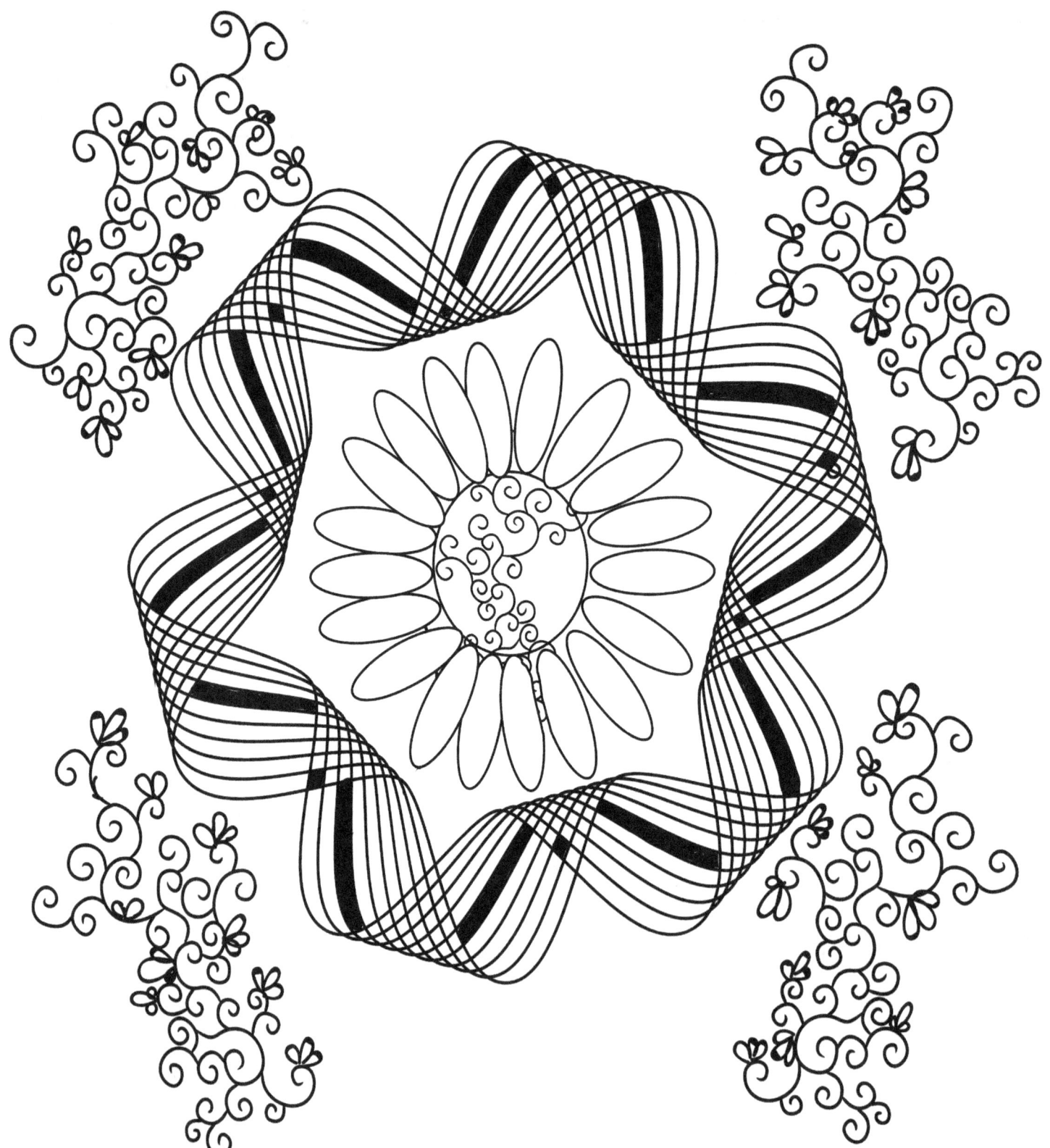

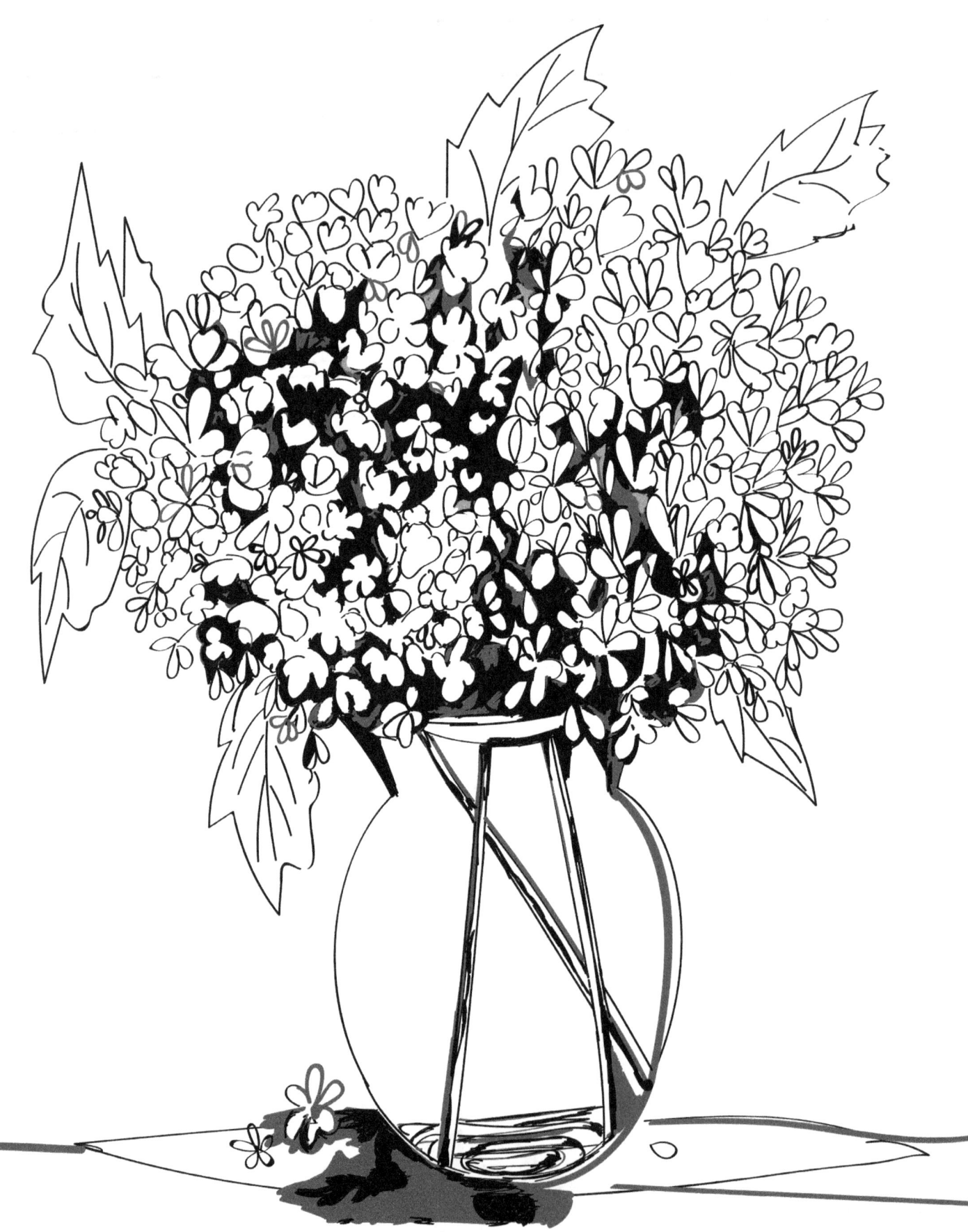

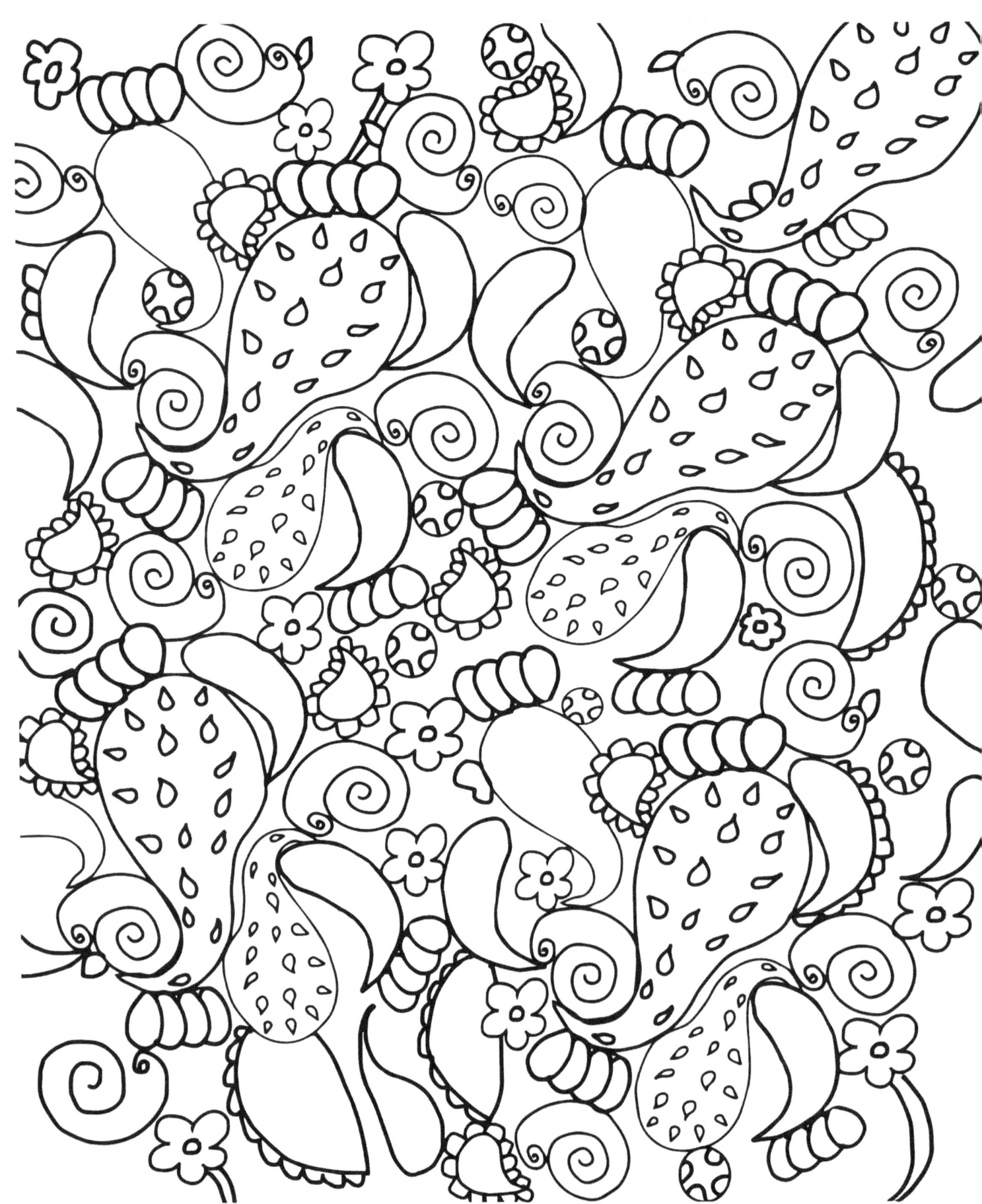

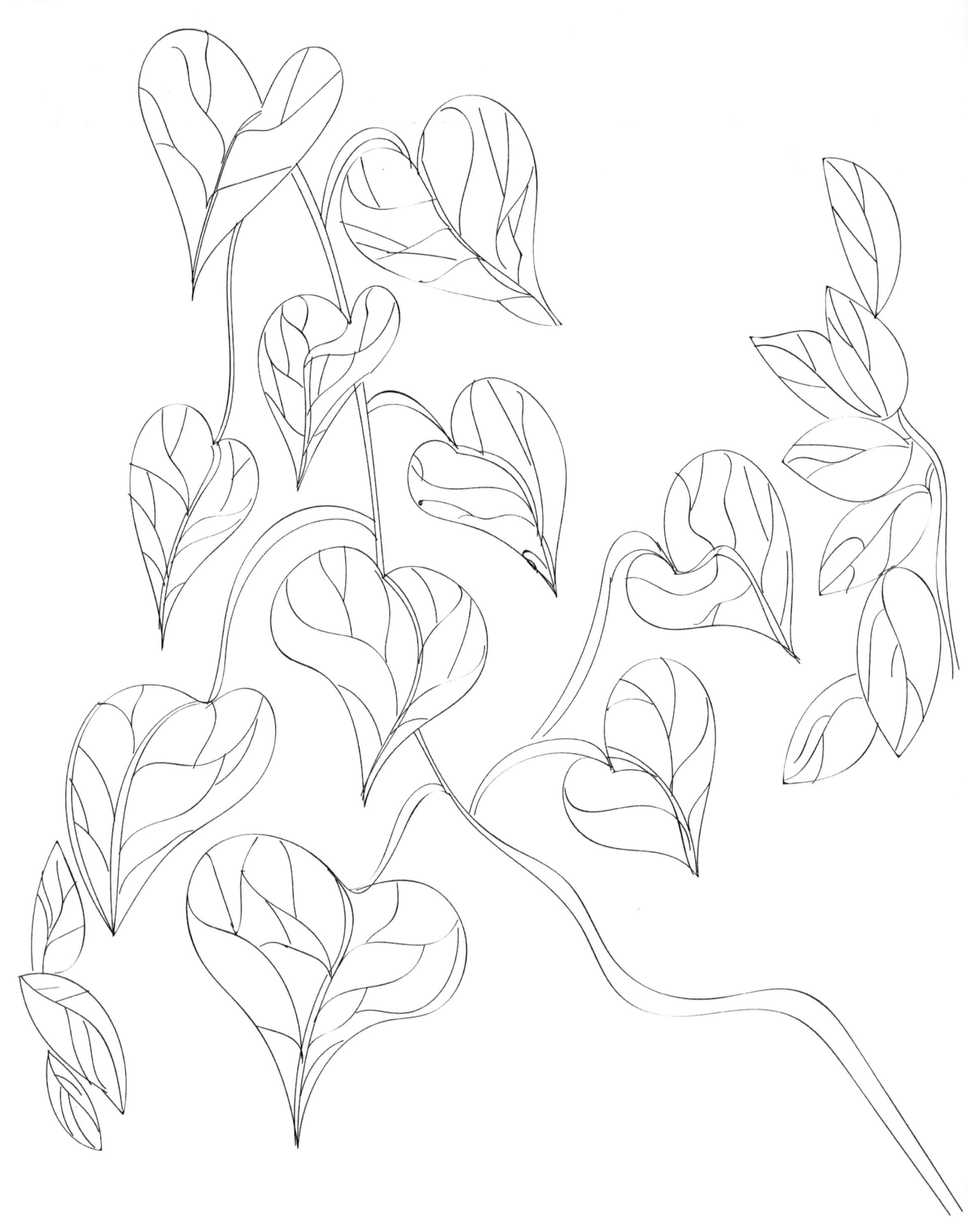

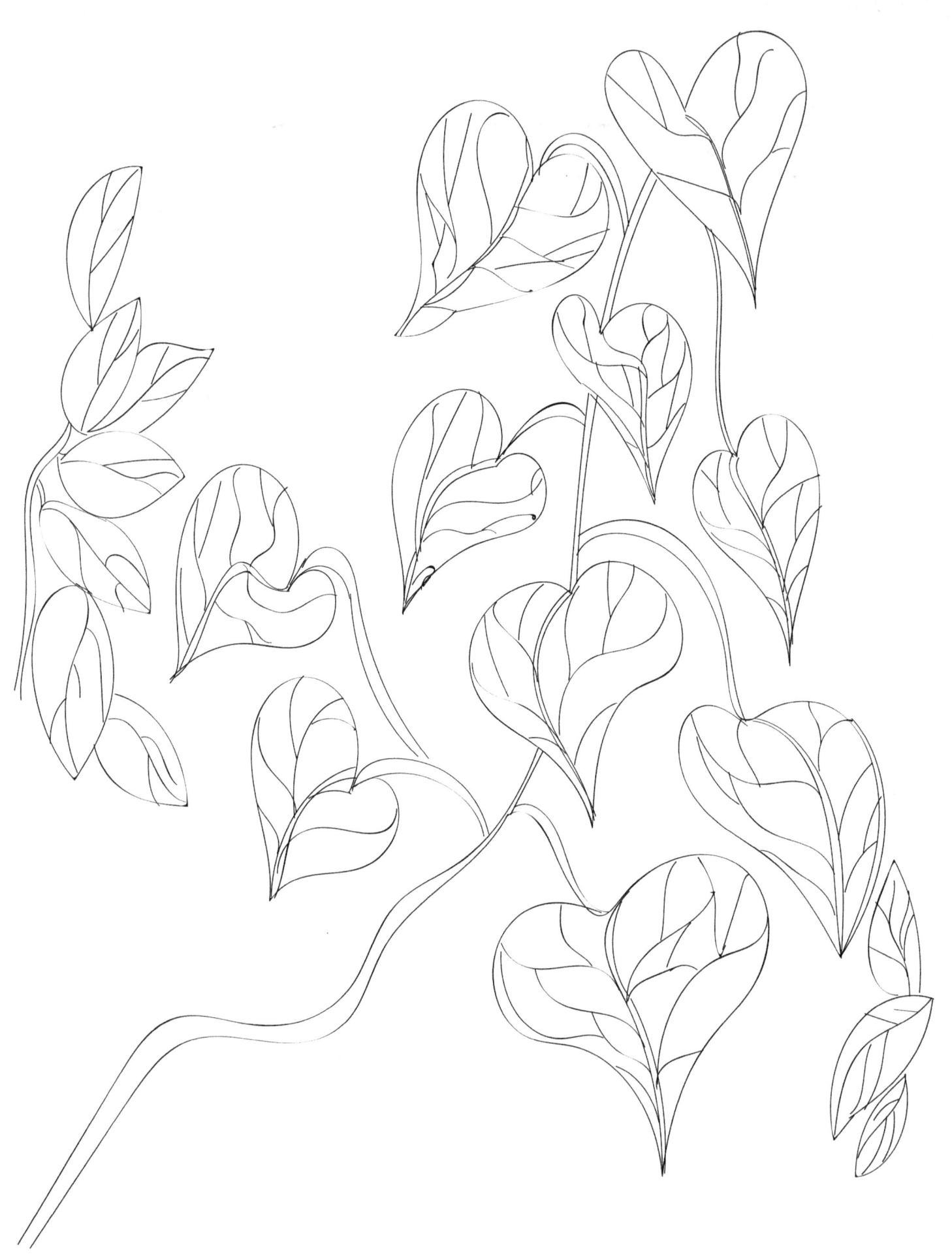

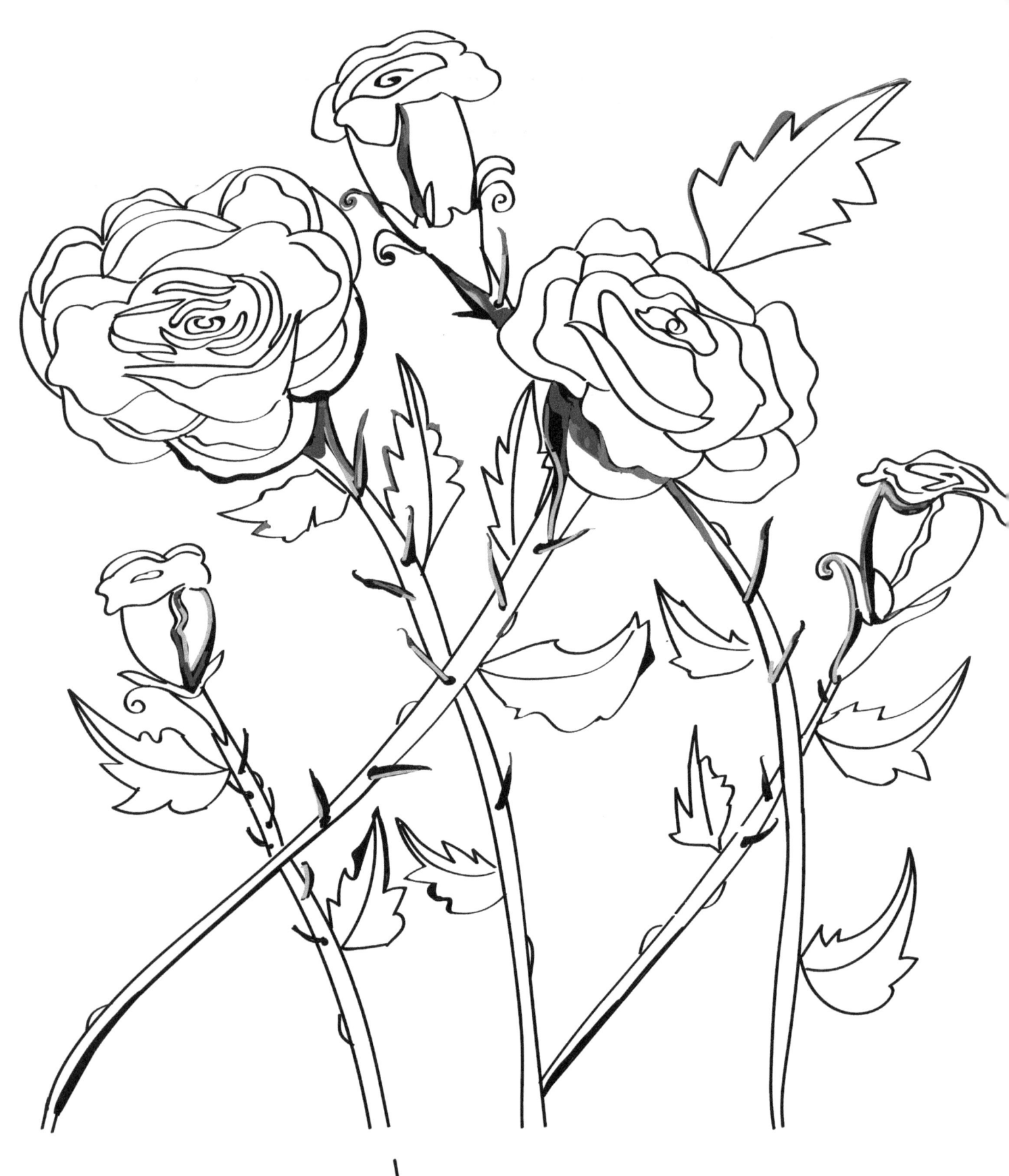

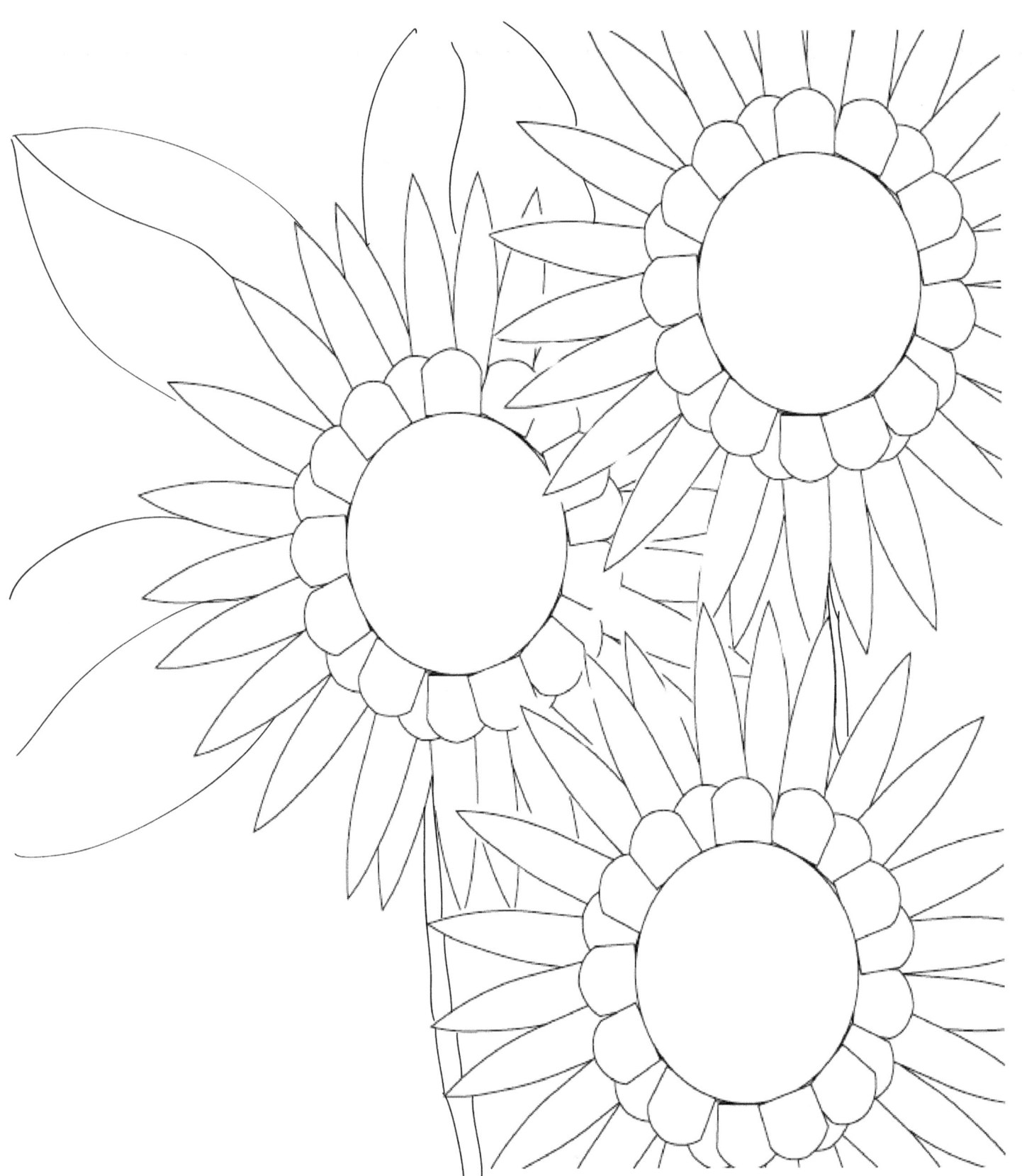

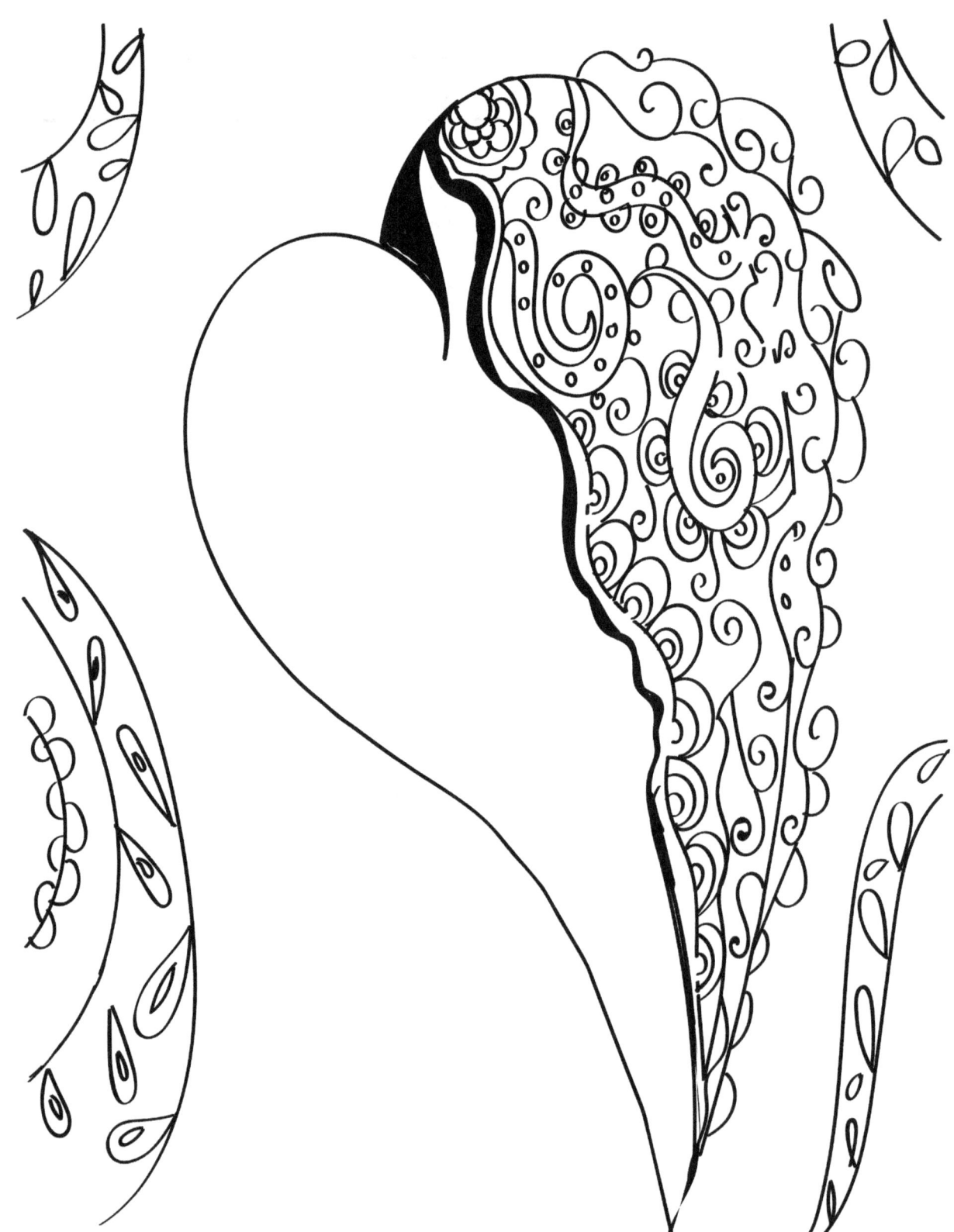

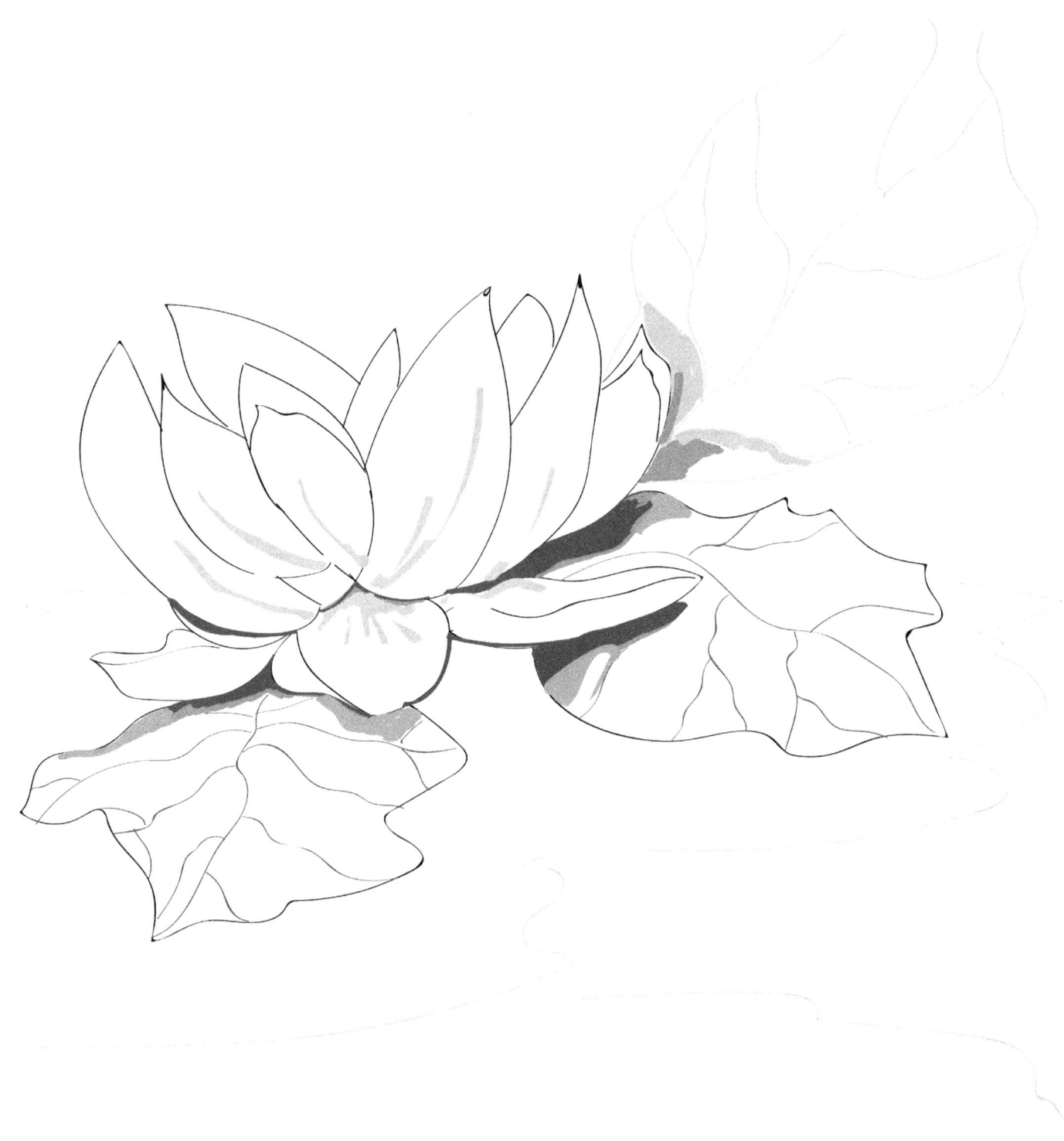

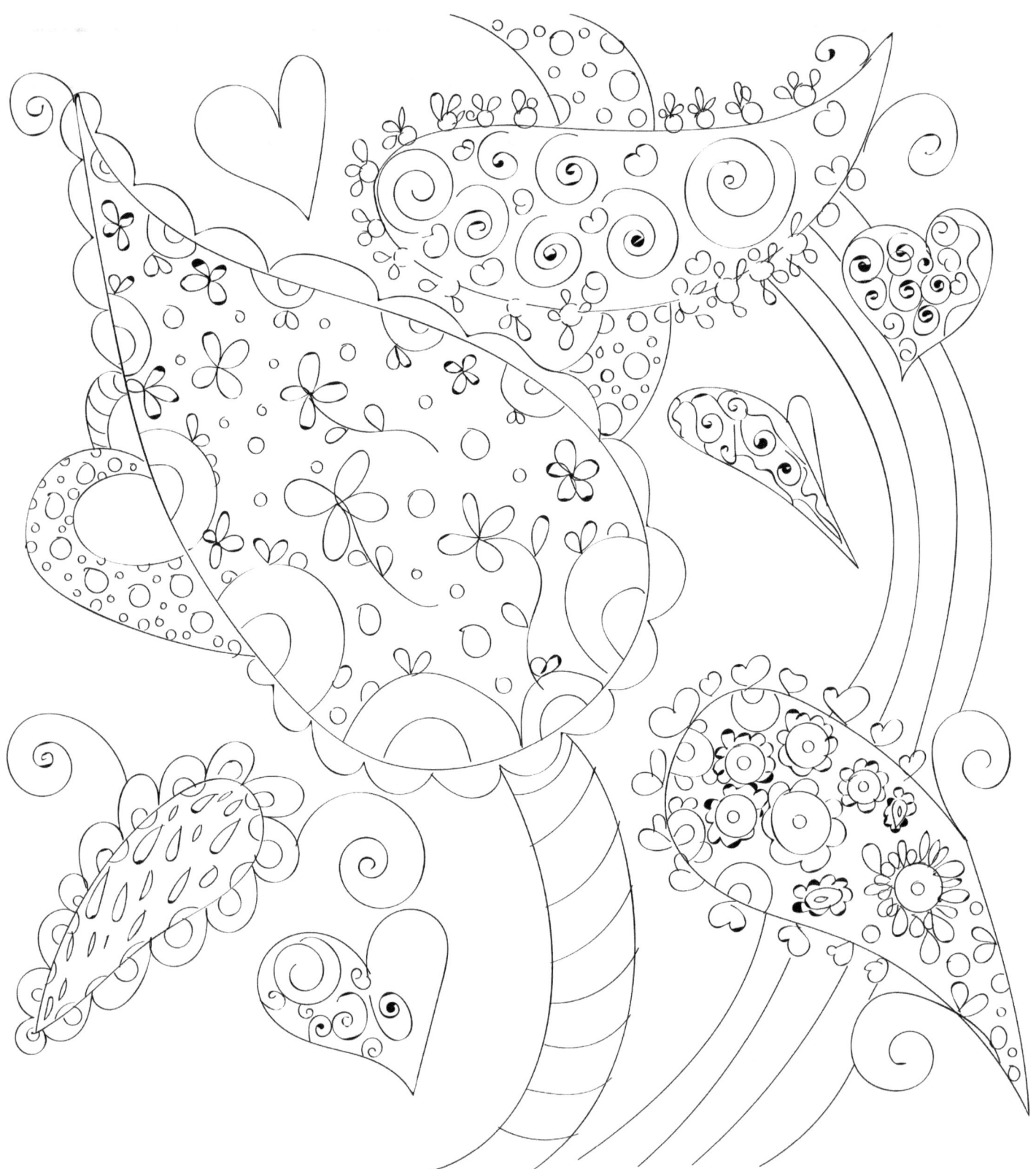

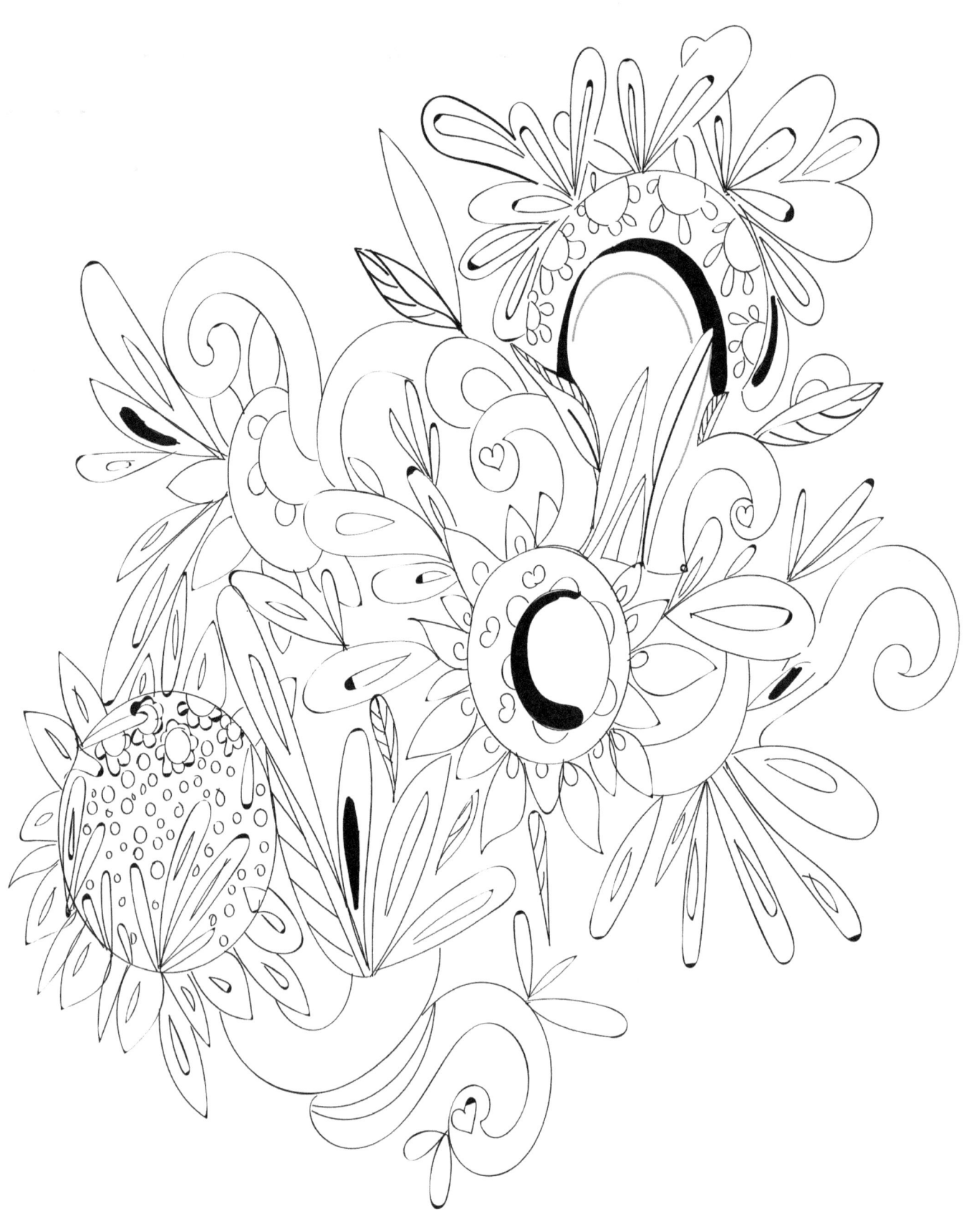

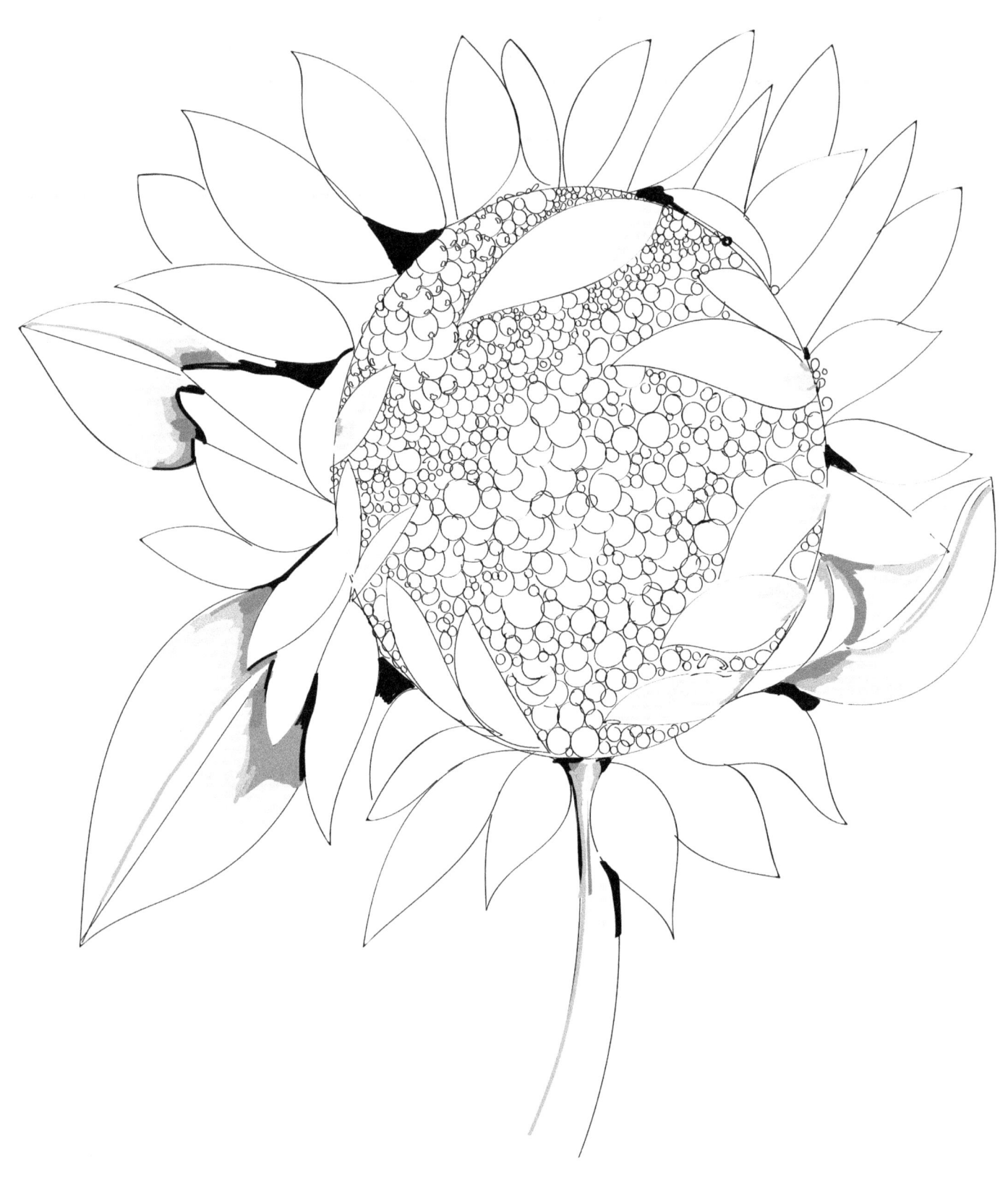

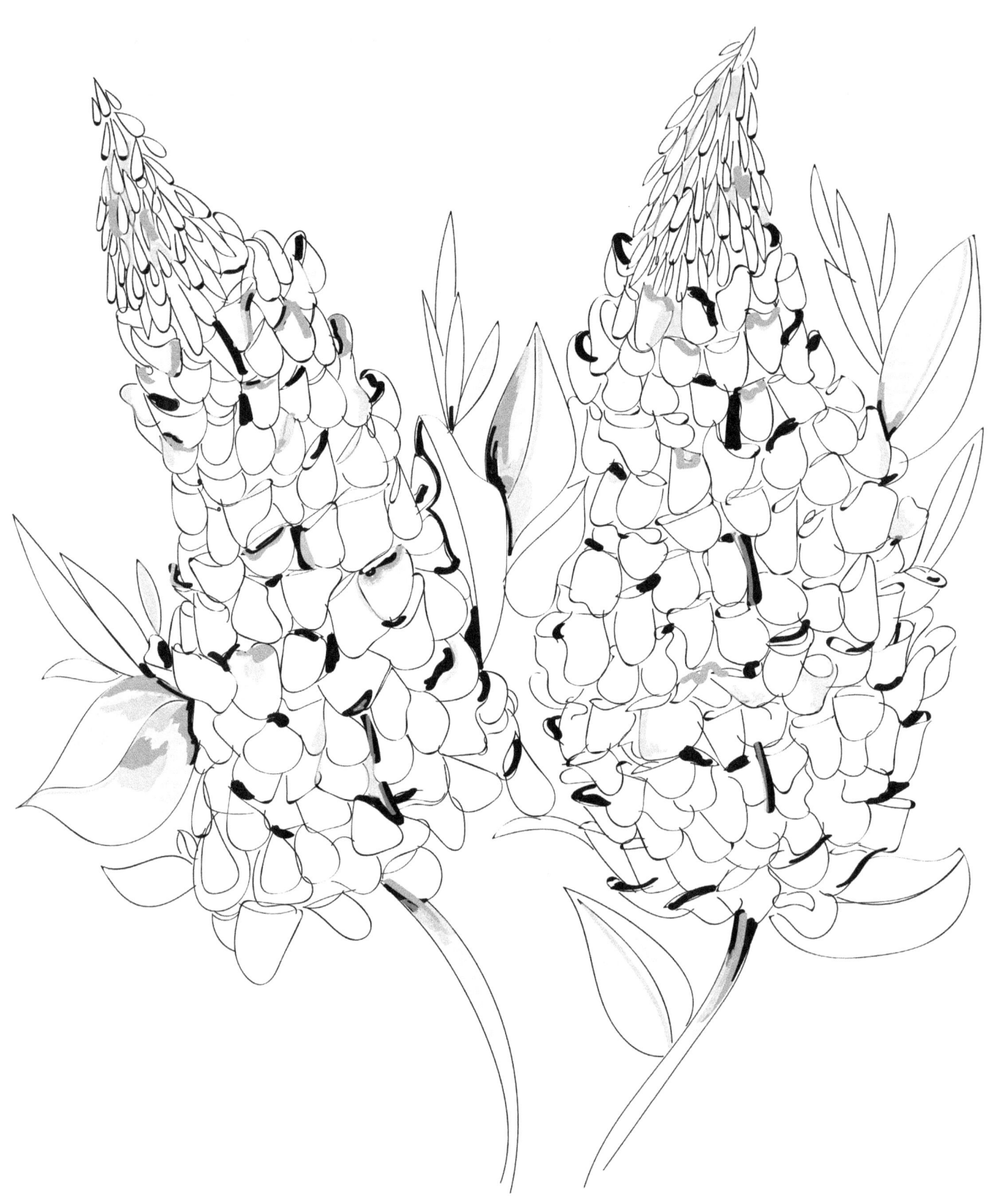

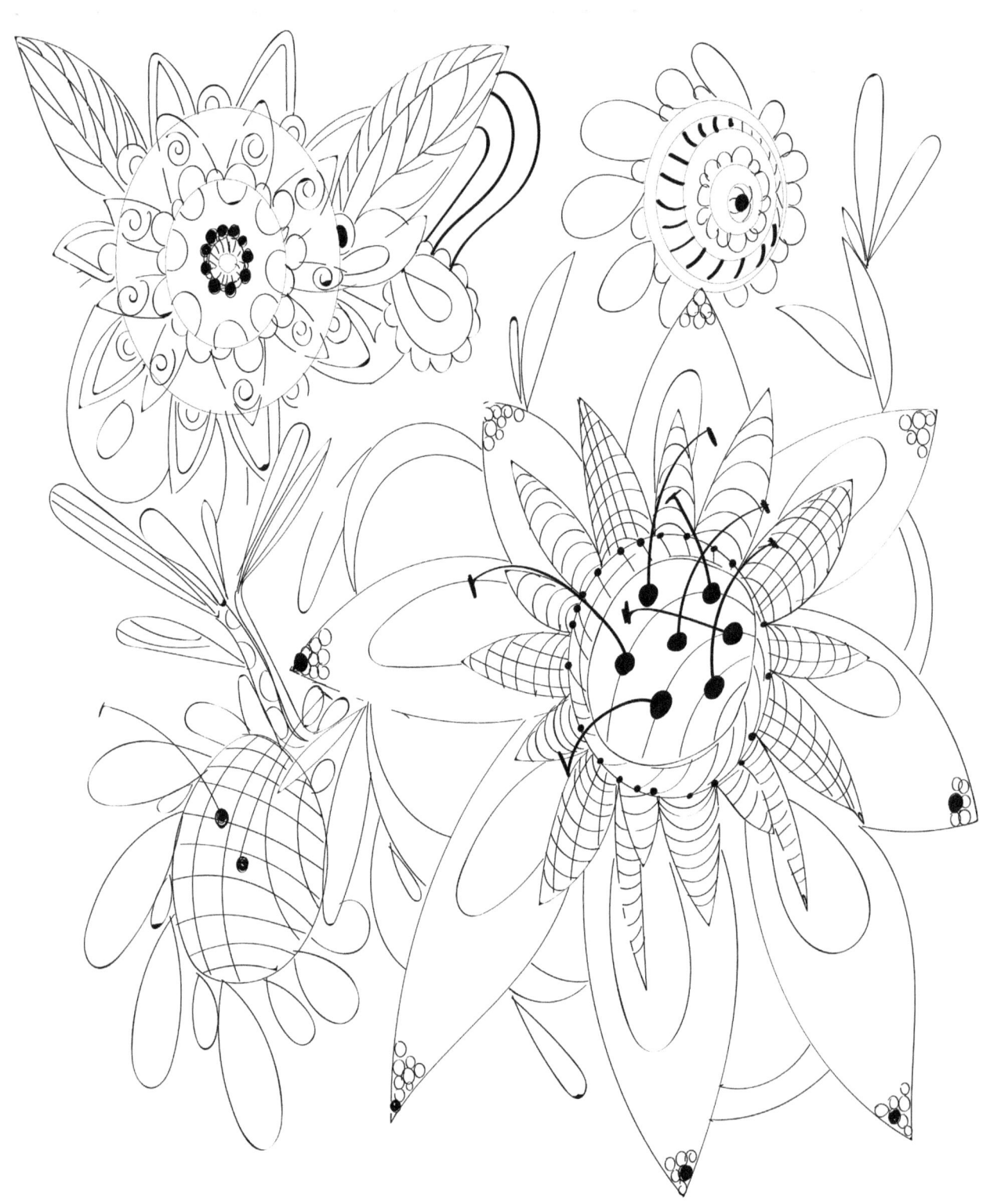

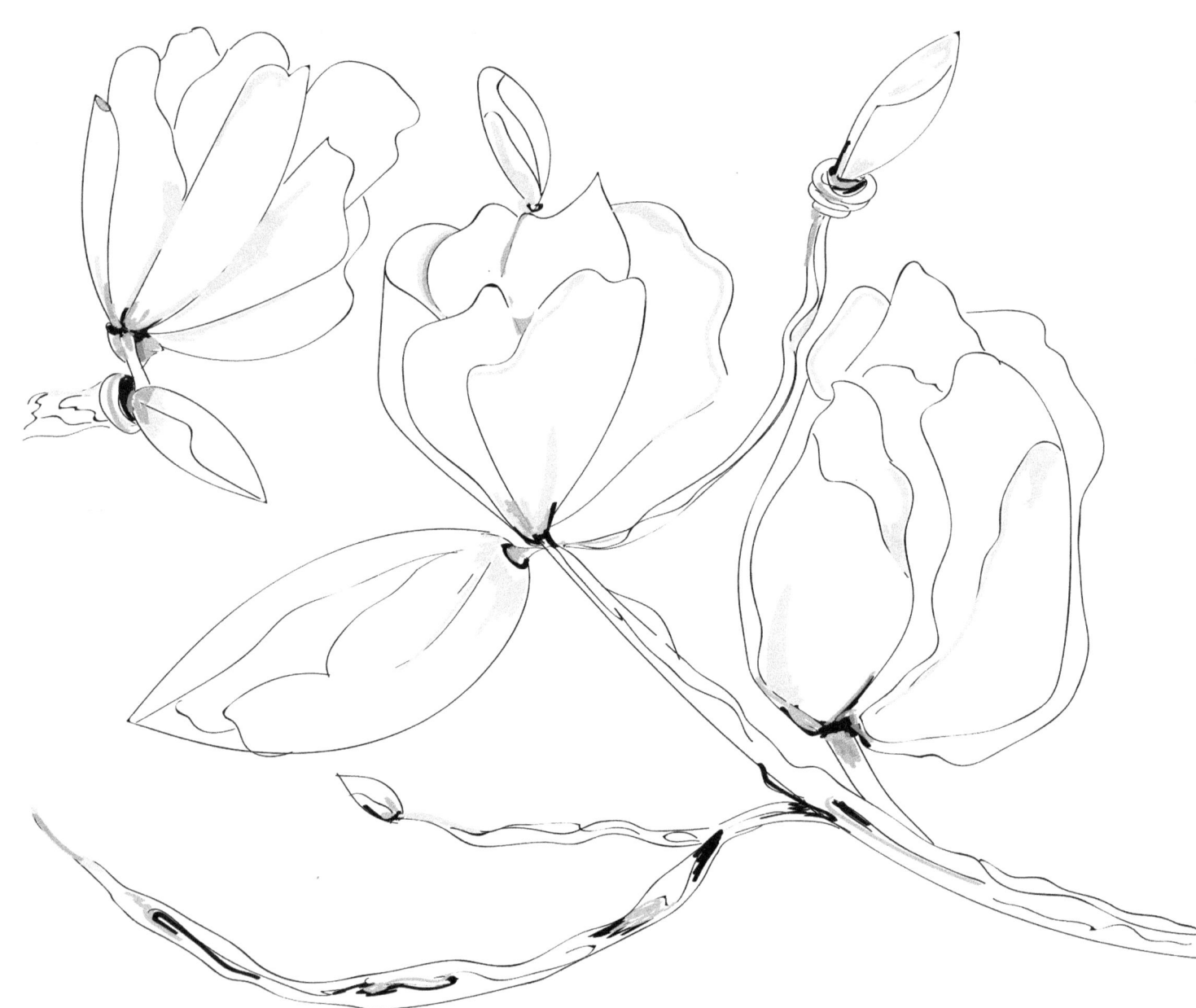

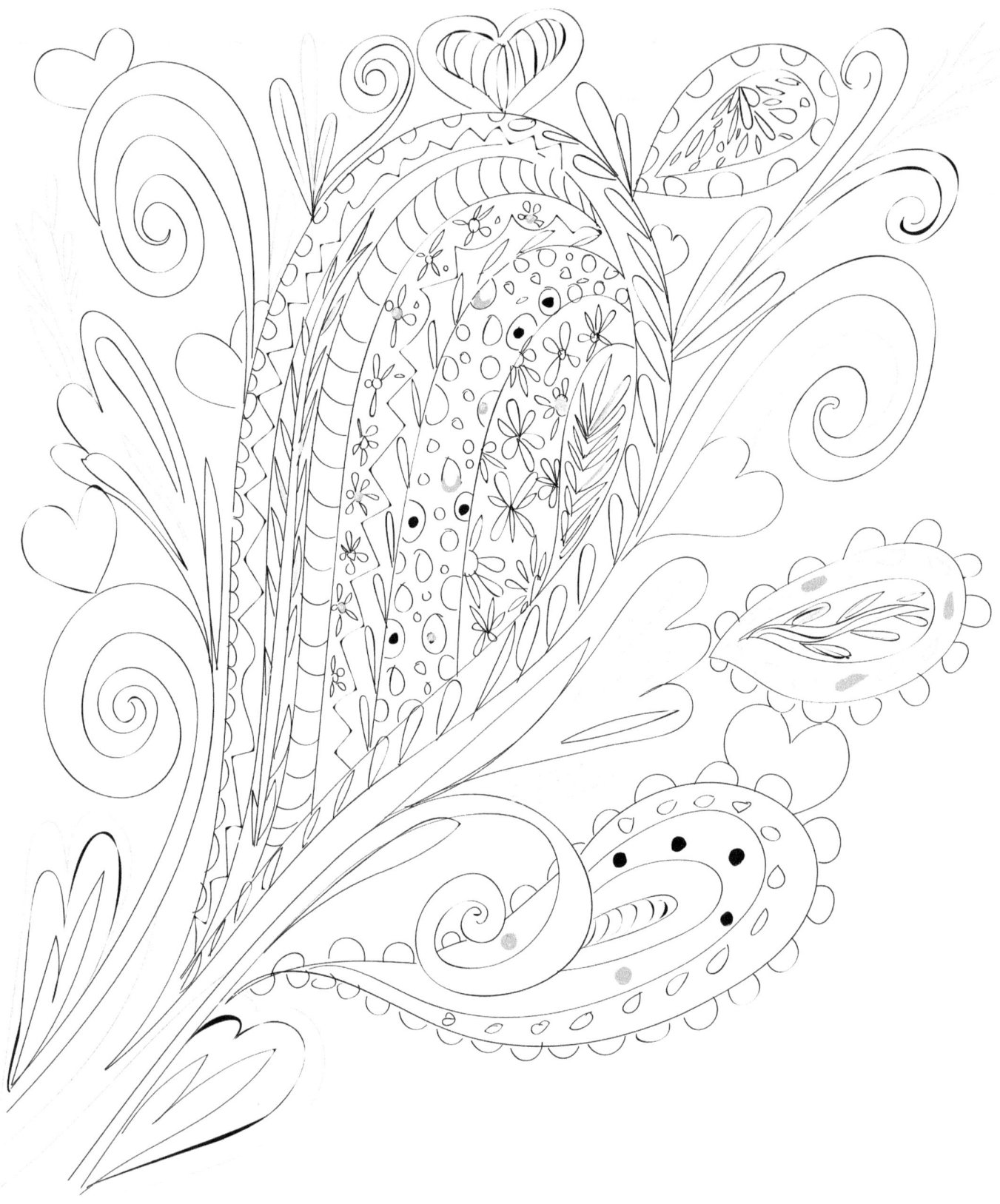

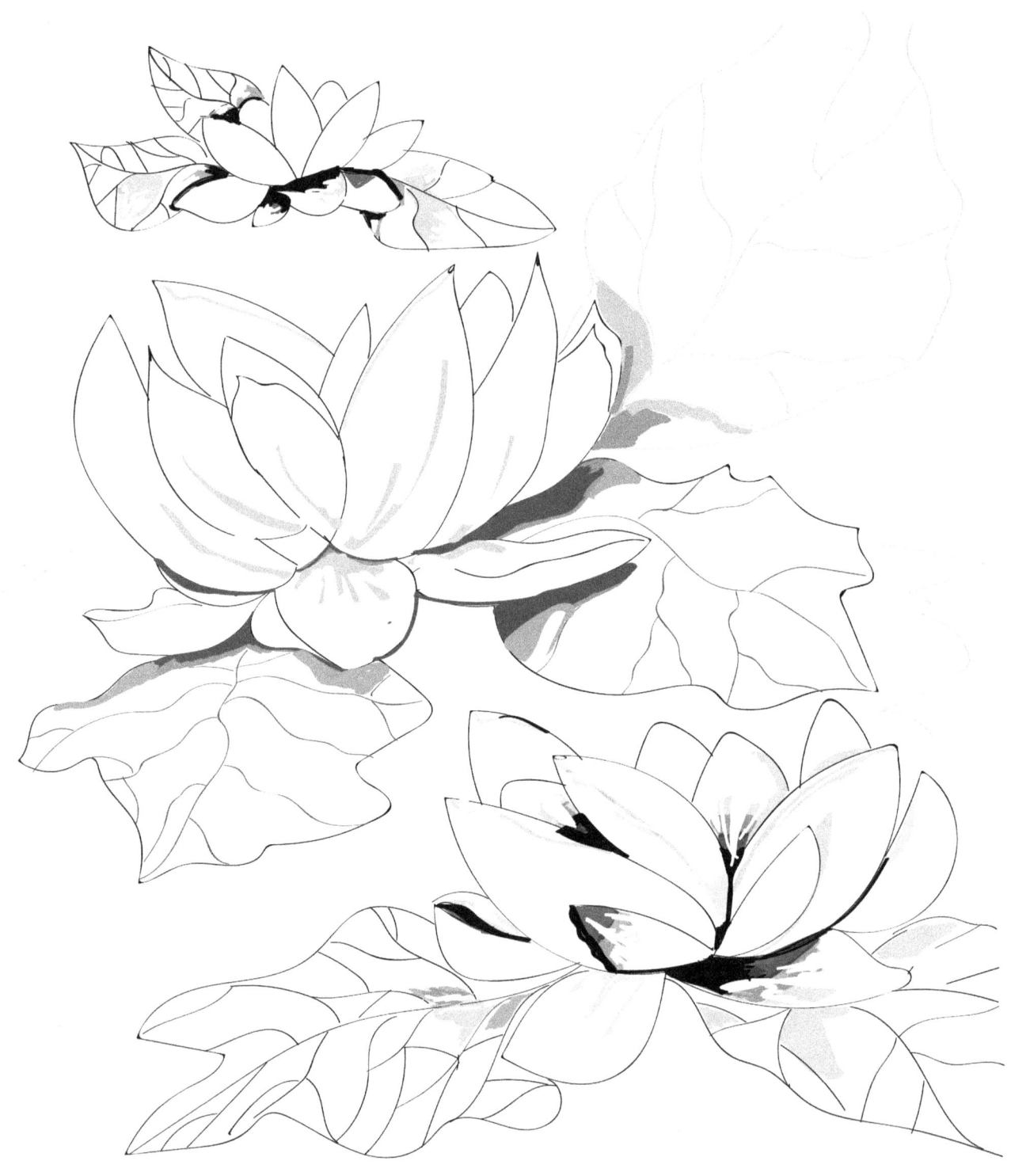

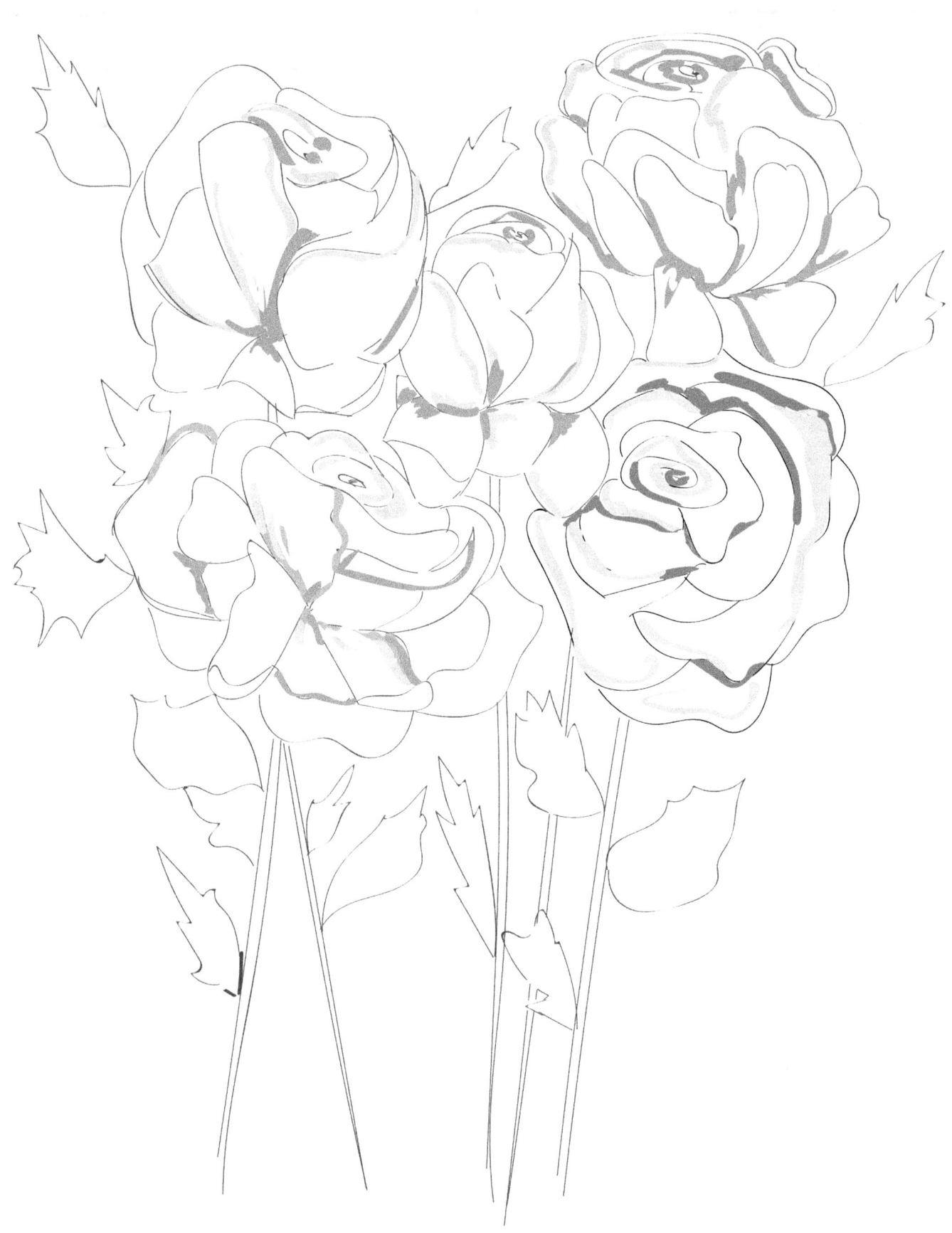

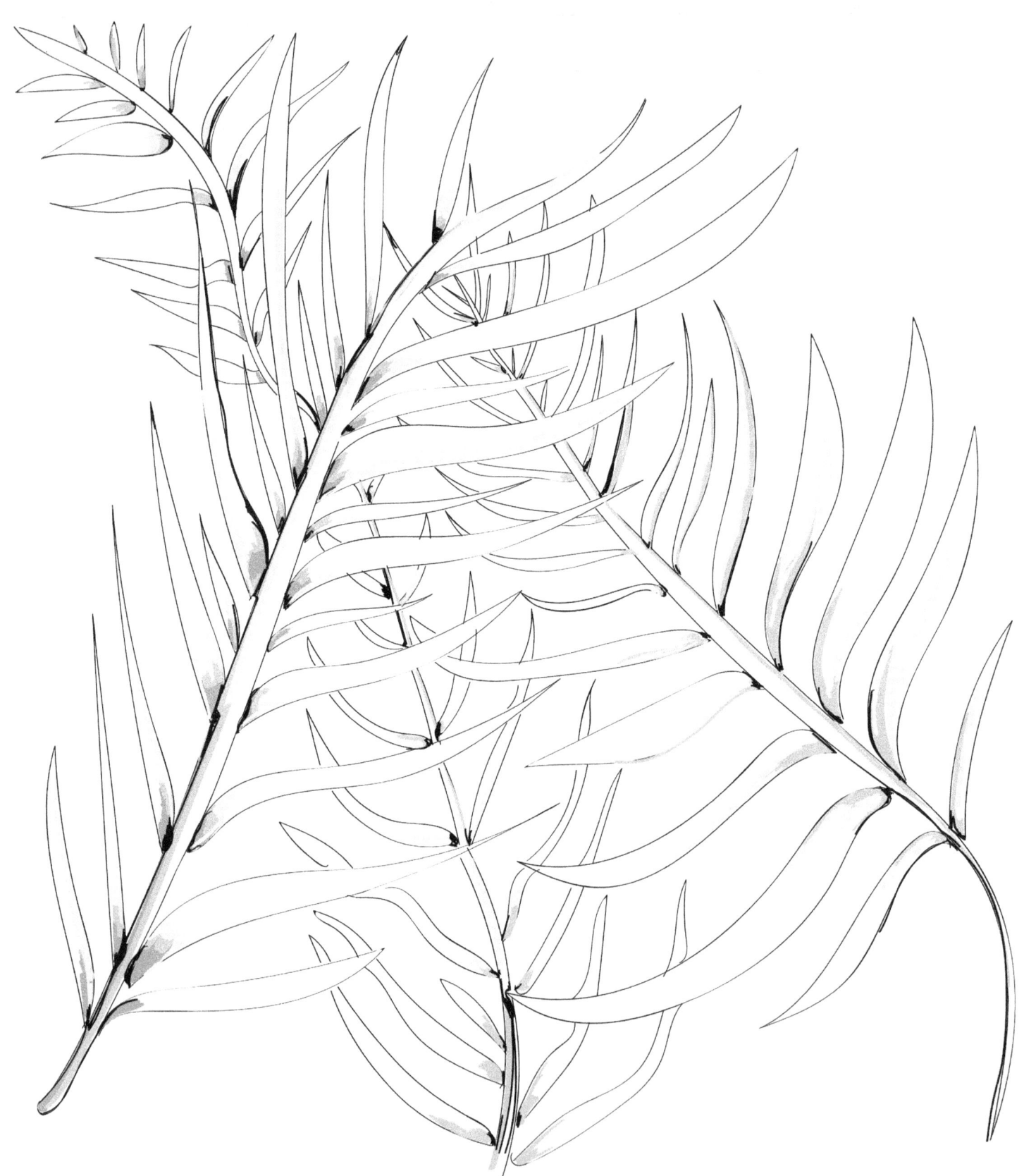

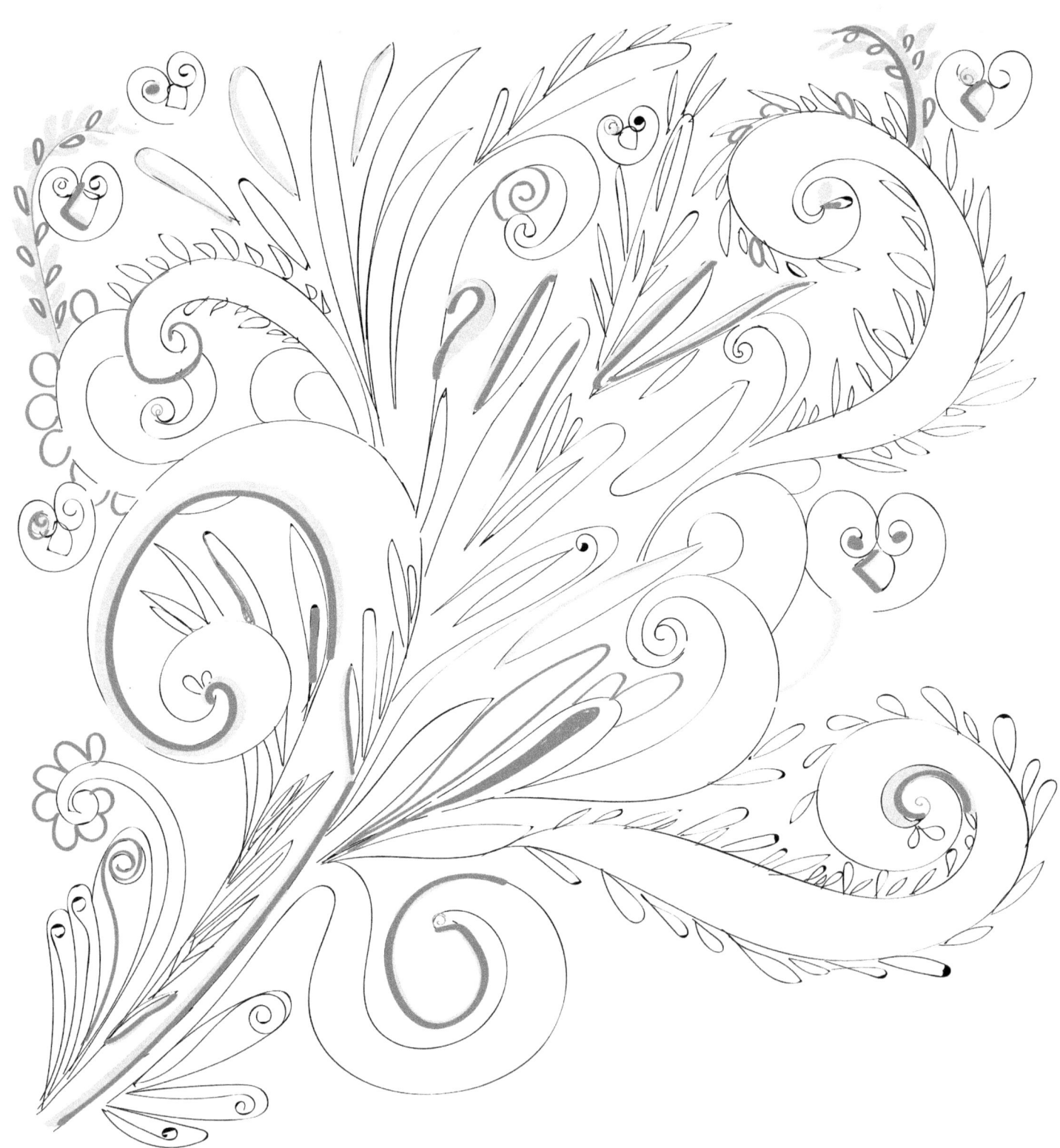

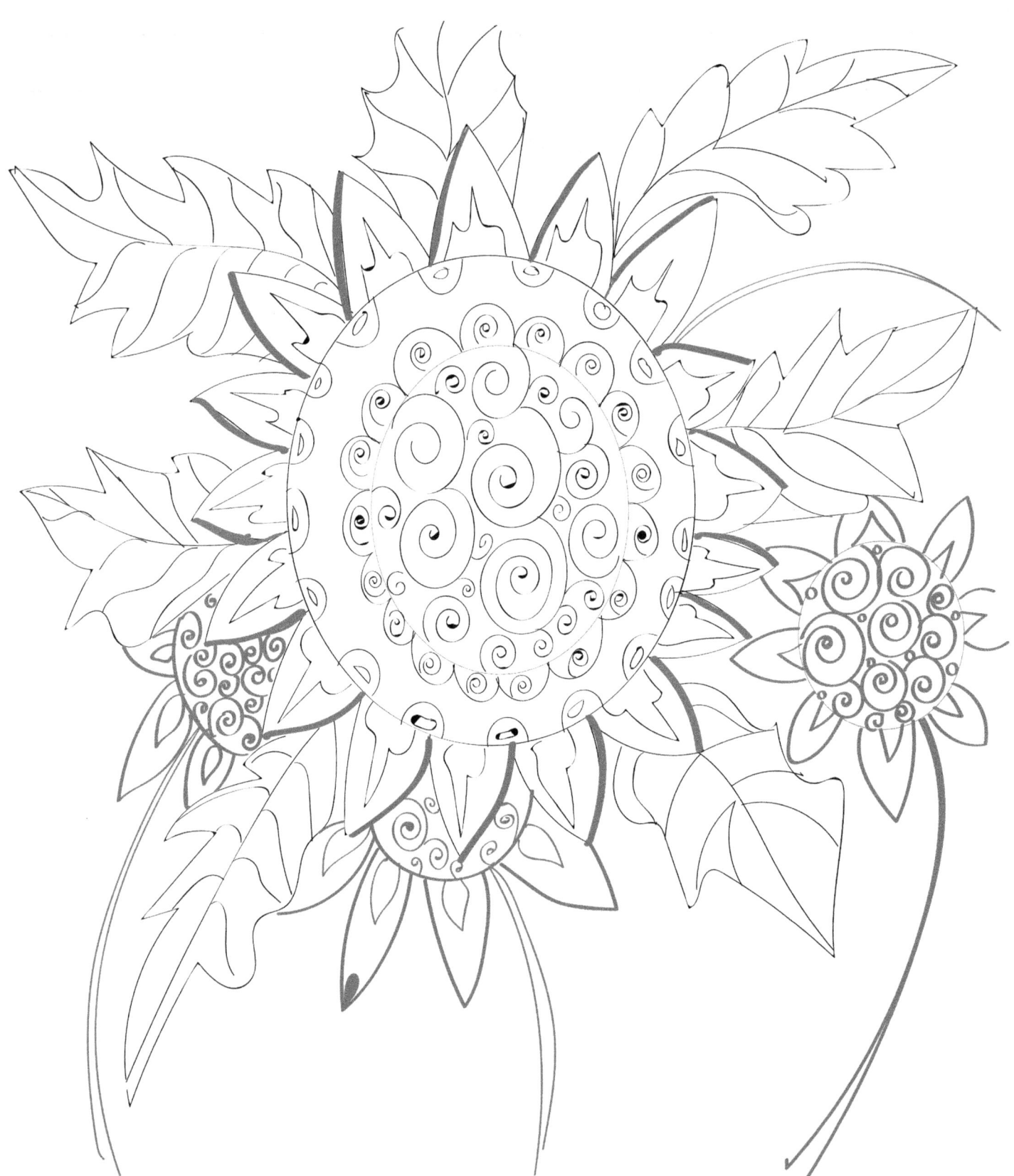

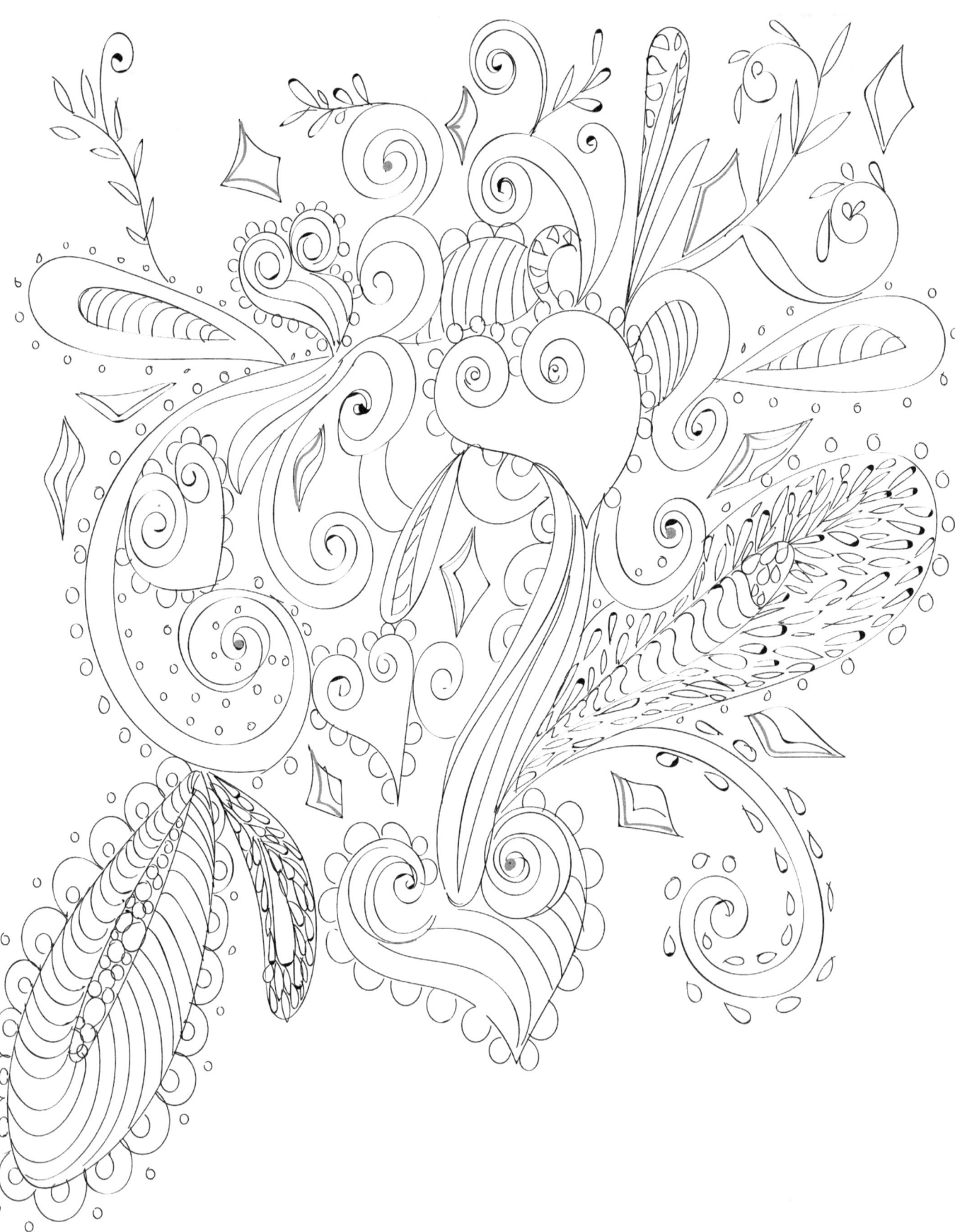

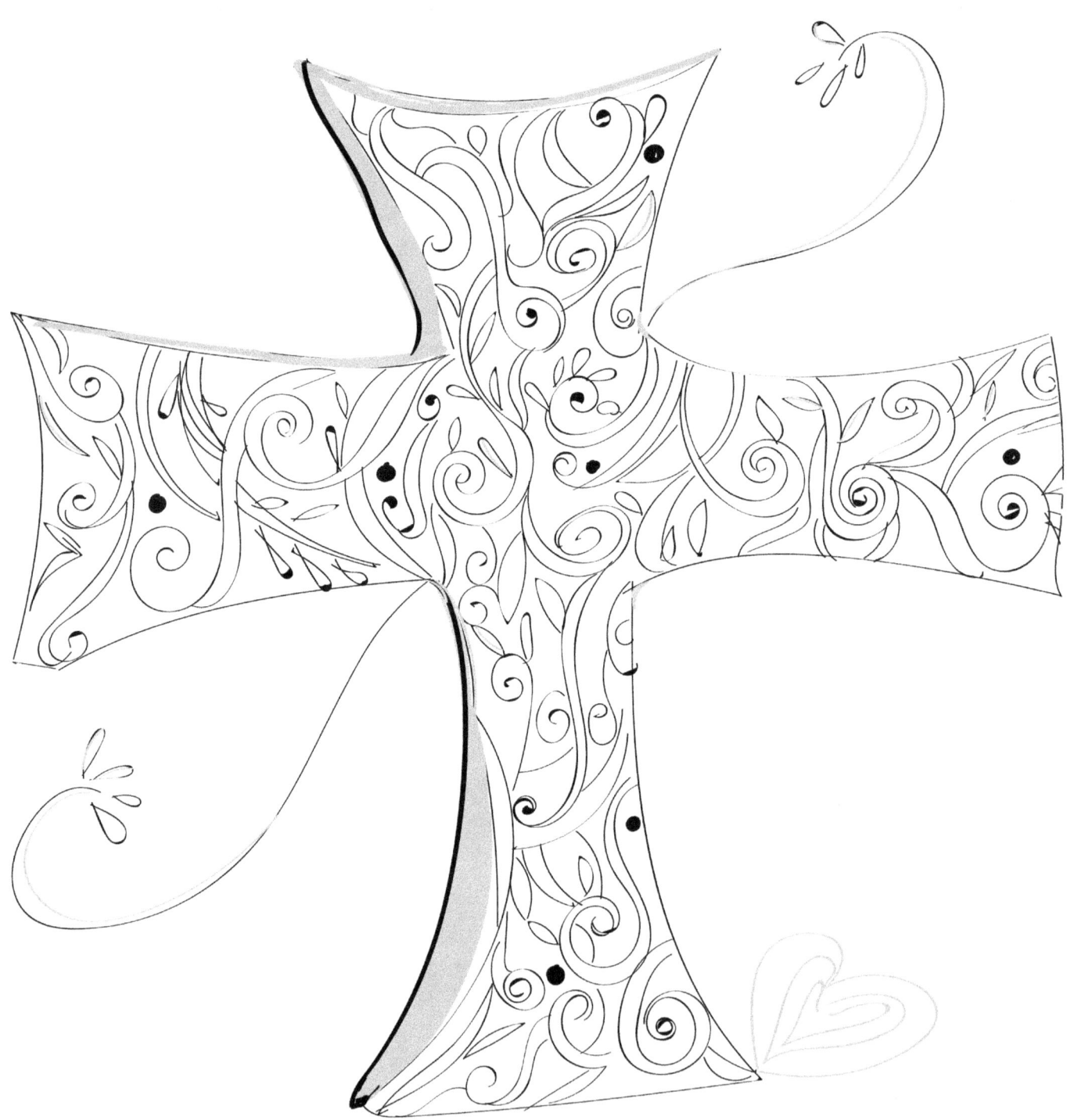

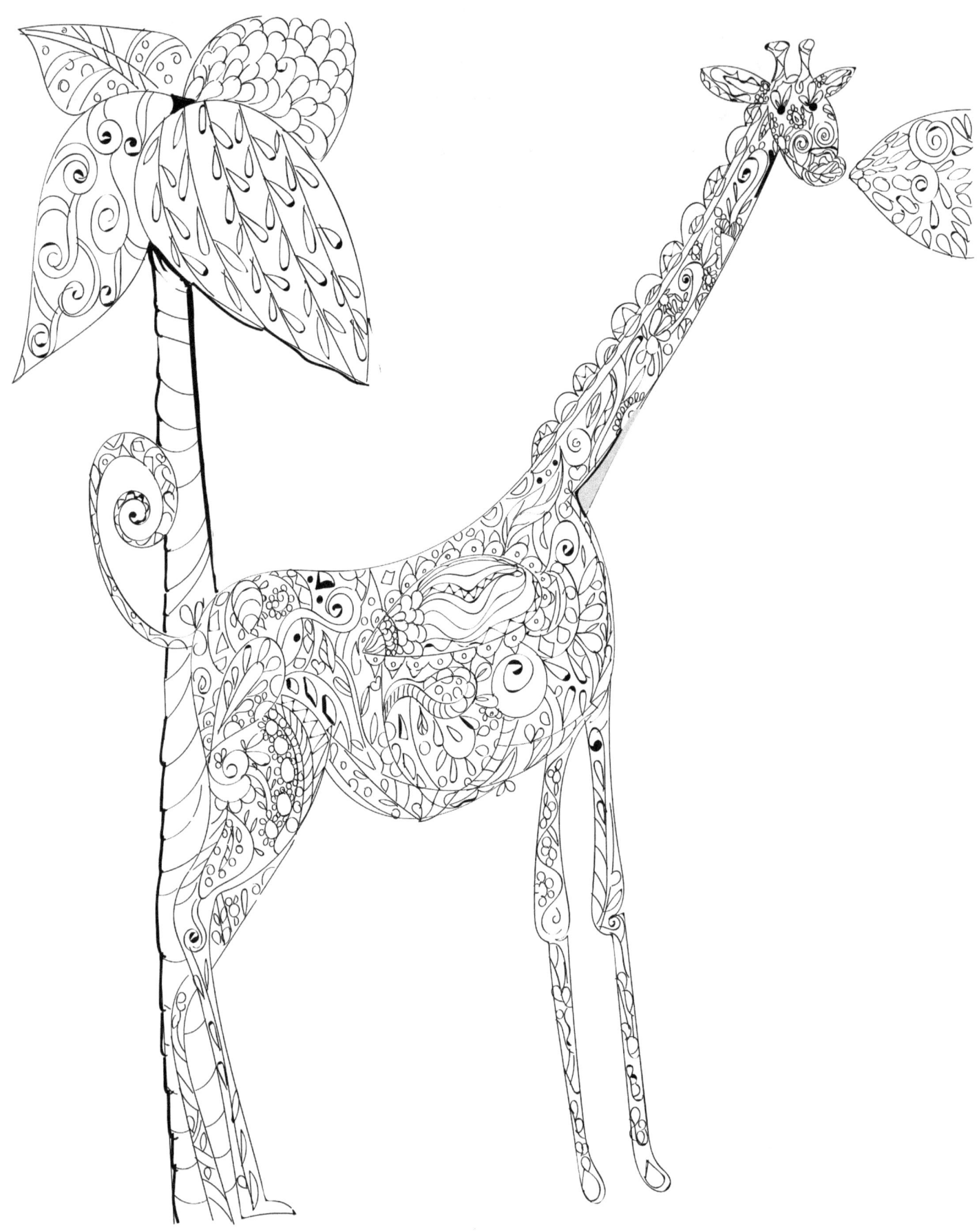

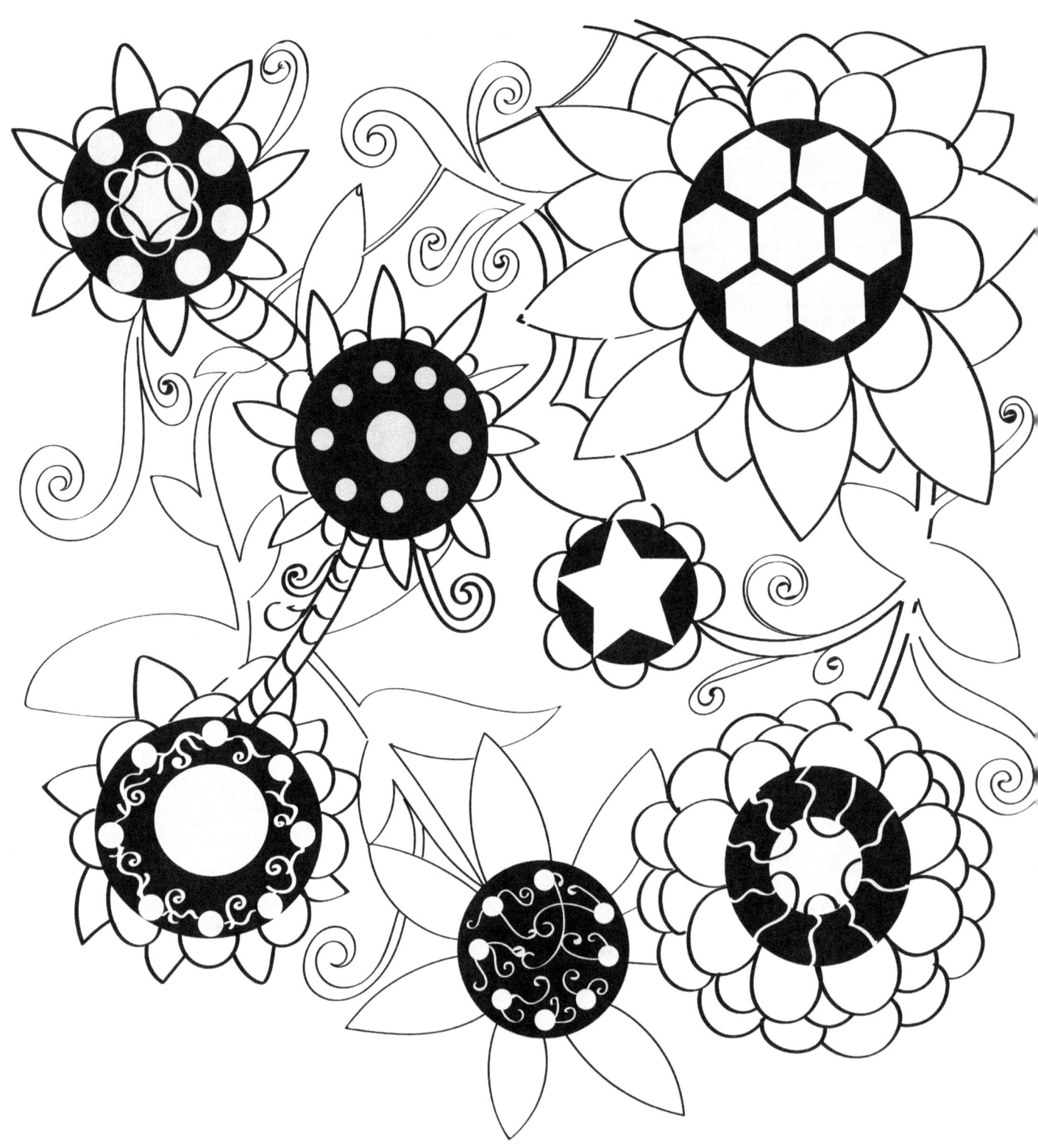

Questions and comments welcomed
wyantagi@gmail.com